# Dawn in Dindustan

*Conducting the Moral Autopsy
of a Nation*

James LaFond is not the author of the term Dindu.
However, Mister LaFond is:
The Discover of Dindustan
The Founder of the sciences of Dinduology,
Dindunomics, Dinduosophy and other cutting edge
anthropological disciplines.
Join the author on his pedestrian quest into the
savage heart of Urban America, otherwise kown as
Dindustan.

A Punch Buggy Book

Cover art by Mescaline Franklin, "House of the
Future," barred by the owner/occupant in early 2016

## Books by James LaFond

### Nonfiction
The Fighting Edge, 2000
The Logic of Steel, 2001
The First Boxers, 2011
The Gods of Boxing, 2011
All Power Fighting, 2011
When You're Food, 2011
The Lesser Angles of Our Nature, 2012
The Logic of Force, 2012
The Greatest Boxer, 2012
Take Me to Your Breeder, 2014
The Streets Have Eyes, 2014

Panhandler Nation, 2014
The Ghetto Grocer, 2014
American Fist, 2014
Don't Get Boned, 2014
Alienation Nation, 2014
In The Chinks of The Machine, 2014
How the Ghetto Got My Soul, 2014
Saving the World Sucks, 2014
Taboo You, 2014
Winter of a Fighting Life, 2014
Narco Night Train, 2014
Into the Mountains of Madness: in [3 volumes], 2014
Incubus of Your Sacred Emasculation, 2014
Breeder's Digest, 2014
The Third Eye, 2015
Modern Agonistics, 2015
By the Wine Dark Sea, 2015
The Pale Usher, 2016
The End of Masculine Time, 2015
War Drums, 2015
A Thousand Years in His Soul: The Poets, 2015
A Thousand Years in His Soul: The Seers, 2015
Of Lions and Men, 2015
Your Trojan Whorse, 2016
On Bitches, 2016
Equidistant Drowning Babies, 2015
The Boned Zone, 2015
A Sickness of the Heart: Part One, 2015
Let the Weak Fall, 2015
If I Were King, 2015
Dark Art of an Aryan Mystic, 2015
Welcome to Harm City: White Boy, 2015
When You're Food: Raw, 2016
The Punishing Art, 2016
Twerps, Goons and Meatshields, 2016
Our Captain, 2016

Stillbirth of A Nation, 2016
America in Chains, 2106
40,000 Years from Home, 2016
The Sardonyx Stone, 2017
Paleface Sunset, 2016
Habitat Hoodrat: Ho Nation, 2016
When Your Job Sucks, 2016
A Once Great Medieval City, 2016
Right on White Time, 2016
A Well of Heroes: One, 2016
A Well of Heroes: Two, 2016
Thriving in Bad Places, 2016
Into Wicked Company, 2016
One Soul Under God, 2016
Under the God of Things, 2016
When Your Job Sucks, 2016
Dawn in Dindustan, 2016
Good Morning Dindustan, 2016
The Hunt for Whitey, 2017
Habitat Hoodrat: Yo Nation, 2016
The Combat Space, 2017
A Dread Grace: One, 2017
The Liver-Eater Reader, 2017
Rubbing Out palefaces, 2017
In Words, 2017
Slave Nation, 2016
I Am White, 2017
The Lies that Bind Us, 2017
Real Heroes, 2017
Aryan Myth, 2017
Why Grownups Suck, 2017
A Dread Grace: Two, 2017
A Well of Heroes: Three, 2017
The Boxer Dread, 2017

**Fiction**

Astride the Chariot of Night, 2014
Sacrifix, 2014
Rise, 2014
Motherworld, 2014
Planet Buzzkill, 2014
Fruit of The Deceiver, 2014
Forty Hands of Night, 2014
Black and Pale, 2014
Daughters of Moros, 2014
Darkly, 2014
This Design is Called Paisley, 2015
Hurt Stoker, 2015
Poet, 2016
Triumph, 2015
Winter, 2015
The Spiral Case, 2016
Hemavore, with S. L. James, 2016
Yusuf of the Dusk, 2017
Beyond the Pale, 2017
RetroGenesis: Day 1, with Erique Watson, 2015
Easy Chair, 2015
Happily Ever Under, 2015
Road Killing, 2015
Fat Girl Dancing, 2015
Buzz Bunny, 2015
T. Spoone Slickens, Inquire, 2015
Dream Flower, 2015
The Song of Jeannot, 2015
Organa, 2015
A Hoodrat Halloween, 2015
Buzz Bunny, 2015
The Consultant, 2015
Reverent Chandler, 2015
He, 2016
Little Feet Going Nowhere, 2016
DoomFawn, 2016

The Jericho Bone, 2016
Ire and Ice, 2016
Night City, 2016
Skulker Jones, 2016
A White Christmas, 2016
Night Song of the Nords, 2017
The Absolvant, 2017
Wendigo, 2017
Sold, 2017
Bad Medicine, 2018
Kettle of Bones, 2019

**Sunset Saga Novels**
Big Water Blood Song, 2011
Ghosts of the Sunset World, 2011
Beyond the Ember Star, 2012
Comes the Six Winter Night, 2012
Thunder-Boy, 2012
The World is Our Widow, 2013
Behind the Sunset Veil, 2013
Den of The Ender, 2013
God's Picture Maker, 2014
Out of Time, 2015
Seven Moons Deep, 2017
WhiteSkyCanoe, 2018

## Table of Contents

# Dawn in Dindustan
## Conducting the Moral Autopsy of a Nation

© 2016 James LaFond

All of my internet reading is directed by my readers who are all more internet-savvy than I, as evidence that they have found this website, which I am told is no small feat. Recently an Israeli reader was discussing urban life in America, a life from which he has removed himself in utmost disgust. He used the term Dindu when describing that sainted and oft martyred segment of the population which has suffered most at the hands of hate-filled capitalists and their burning of 153 Baltimore locations in April 2015. I wrote him back and inquired if he had just coined an ethnographic term that was a play on the name Hindu and poking fun at those people who are often moved to say, "But I din do nothin,'" as they stand at the scene of their most recently committed crime, seemingly bemused at the fact that the

11

responding officer is not at all bemused as to the agent of this particular criminal act.

My friend informed me that Dindu is a commonly understood term among internet-savvy folk who are not endeared with those who din do nothin'. Having just finished Paleface Sunset, it seems to me that a nation should be named not according to its false ideals but according to the people for whom it exists. Rome was named for the Romans—not for the Greeks who toiled educating their brutish children, nor for the Germans who guarded the Roman head of state, nor for the Armenian dancing girls that diverted the lead-brained attention of the head of state [the Romans in retrospect did have a lot to recommend them, for instance, in ancient Rome, Kardashian girls were shackled to a bedpost and had zero influence on the formation of public opinion].

So, what does one name a nation that has lost its identity?

We can strike united from the hood ornament of the cab of state.

As for America, I've always resented being identified with a medieval charlatan who just happened to publicize the existence of that which had been in existence longer than his species.

Therefore, I shall henceforth refer to the nation that owns me according to that martyr people who are held in highest esteem by the functionaries who drive the cab of state.

Well, Paleface, its Monday morning, welcome to Dindustan.

# 'I'm Fed Up'
## Little Mark Among the Swarms of Dindustan

© 2016 James LaFond

I've been living in "The Hood" for twenty years, Greenmount and Twenty-fifth, and at this point I'm fed-up, an angry, little white man sick of being hunted. I've heard the same shit so many times for so long I could do a voice over for the autobiography of that degenerate race: "Whatchyou got white boy? Yo, shortyshortshort where you goin'? Yo, Cracker, this is our shid up in hea! Yo got some money fo me whiteboy? Yo, bitch-ass whiteboy, you lookin' at me? White bitch! Go-on you muvaficin' white bitch!"

You know, I'm sick of it. I don't care if you don't work, collect welfare, get high and throw all of your negro trash on the sidewalk and make the world ugly for the rest of it. But is it too much to ask to keep your hands to yourself? Come on! I'm a little guy, five feet tall, barely. And I like my freedom. I know from experience that using a knife is just a way of handing your ass to the State's Attorney. I tried fighting, God knows I tried—what a disaster. Christ, their teenagers tower over me. I'm smaller than their twelve-year-olds, a little white ape in the land of giant chimps and silver backs. And they attack in swarms, five niggers and me, six niggers and me, seven niggers and me, too many niggers to count while you're getting your lights punched out and me. Now the mother fuckers are carrying knives.

I honestly think the only answer is genocide—that the lot of them need to be herded together and roasted in a fucking oven!

Now, the other day, I walk around the corner and this twelve-year-old kid puts a steak knife in my face and says, "Give it up, yo."

First of all, I'm not a fucking yo, alright. Second of all, I've learned that I can't trade punches with these assholes. I did did wrestle in high school and was pretty good. So I grabbed his hand and put it behind his back and did a trip and dropped his monkey ass onto the pavement and took the knife. I punched him a few times while he was down there and went on my way.

I worked last week driving a friend back and forth to a jab in Ocean City—earned forty bucks a day—he's the executive chef for a restaurant chain. I love this new car—put two thousand miles on it last week. Went up to Northern PA to visit a friend who finally got fed-up with all of this Negro States of Their America bullshit and is living in a small town and loving life. My problem is I can't sell the house and the hell if I'm going to let the government section-eight it to these fucking savages. That's my family heritage. It's not going to become a heroin shooting gallery or a crackhouse. The day may come for me to love life in a small town. For today, having this car is my salvation and I'm glad to give you a ride, brother."

*Mark, who offered me a ride when he saw me heading out to the county with my Caucasium umbrella cane, declined my offer of five dollars for the ride, but did accept $3 for gas money when he dropped me off at the gym on a stormy late spring yesterday.*

# 'A Very Effective Deterrent'
## B on the Use of Dogs for Warding Off Hoodrats

Fortunately for your veteran friend, dogs owned by whites naturally tend to hate hoodrats. It's essential to train them to avoid picking up food from the ground or taking it from strangers, since the first thing you do with a problem dog owned by a potential victim is to poison it (Arabs here do that before stealing from Jewish farmers.) Also it's good to have 2-3 dogs so that they can pack up; one dog is easy to subdue with a long pole or a Tazer, although I doubt ghetto blacks have the motivation or discipline-but you can never be too sure. You have to make sure they are not restricted in their movement; unleashed is the way to go, although cops are a problem if you're walking with them off the leash.

I myself have a small border collie/kelpie mix and a massive Central Asian shepherd. The former does the scouting and thinking, the latter guards. I keep them off the leash around the house/settlement, and often take them for runs-the little one runs out about 30-50 meters to scout, the big one sticks within 2-5 meters to bodyguard. They also escort my 2 1/2 year old son around the settlement when he wanders around.

In general, a big, properly bred dog is a very effective deterrent if trained properly, a liability/weakness if not.

# On the Ocean of Extinction

**Paleface Sunset: A Guide to Cultural Resistance in the Age of Felonious Paperback – June 7, 2016 by James LaFond (Author)**

"Befoe da rise of Dindustan, en da conversion of Whitey's spy satellites to da task a broadcastin' hip hop globally—showd out to our smart fuckin' Chinese bruthas foe dat—twenty-fo, seven up in dey Mozart shit, so even dem survivaless cracka's up in da I'llaskya got to hea—dey almose decided ta fight. Fortunately fo us dey didn' read dis hateful shid hea."

"I tell ya doe, I do miss dem white bitchez—oughta fine some Hindu muthafuca to make some a dem shorties in a tess tube.

-Dramaskal "Be Bangin' Bitchez" Creed, Secretary of State, 2048

19

The author of this book is an apparently insane boxing coach and stick-fighter, who does not accept the truism that all that is wrong with the world is the fault of working class men of European descent, and that, instead, international bankers and the politicians who dance upon their puppet strings have targeted the myriad Caucasian Cultures and extant, pan-cultural notions of masculinity for extinction in an attempt to remove from the globalist path the one obstacle that might prevent the final evolution of the human race into a hive of mono-cropped primates.

Although the author is clearly insane and probably just needs to try a new flavor of stage one baby food to silence his anti-American musings, he is an entertaining crackpot. Therefore, the Council on Un-American Opinion has recommended this rampant screed as a means of ferreting out the traitors in your midst. Simply read aloud from this hate-filled rant, and should any who listen nod in agreement at any point, report them to the Council on Un-American Opinion at a University near you.

# At the Dindustan Theater: 1
**The Adjustment Bureau, with Matt Damon, Based on Phillip K. Dick's Story, The Adjustment Team**

© 2016 James LaFond

Billed as a "Smart, Stylish thriller" and "Based on a story by the legendary Phillip K. Dick," I was looking forward to a pleasurable diversion when I put in this fairly recent Dinduwood offering, crossing my fingers that it would not turn into work—then dawned the fact that I reside in the ever-expanding Dindustan continuum—I noticed that a sagely concerned, observant character, oozing empathy, and wisdom for the befuddled white man, just happened to be a young black man. I knew then and there that Matt Damon's charter would be edified and saved from the damnation of other whites... and it was so.

Look, I like black heroes.

I write black heroes.

I wrote a character as a black quantum physicist.

And no, not everything in Dinduwood revolves around this one morality drive.

Emily Blunt's character had to be inserted—instead of the wife of Dick's story, The Adjustment Team—to have a forbidden love affair to keep women in the movie seats.

Matt Damon's character, instead of being a regular guy with a shit job and a worse boss, must be the next JFK, poised to save the world, but is just as stupid and clueless as the average guy, keeping the average guy in his seat, feeling better about being average.

However, as with most of Dick's stories and most science-fiction of the era, human racial divisions are rarely mentioned and rarely important, with characters usually assumed to be Caucasian. Now, with this story, one can forgive the casting director for replacing the black dog who empathizes with the officer clerk for a black man who empathizes with the future leader of the free world. But, why does this sainted character have to be the only black character?

Cannot he have at least one other black team member?

Can there not be a negative black character?

Could we have a single clueless black character?

Do they all have to be masterminds?

How come all of the white male characters are either dupes like the protagonist or villains?

I find this kind of propagandistic casting as offensive as I found watching 1930s movies as a boy, in which every black person was depicted as a good-natured imbecile.

However, in light of the fact that there is only one casting agent in Dinduwood, I suppose I should get used to it.

# 'Only the Living Can Kill the Dead'

**At the Dindustan Theater: Feature 2— Abraham Lincoln, Vampire Hunter by Seth Grahame-Smith**

© 2016 James LaFond

This movie, based on the Novel by Seth Grahame-Smith, who had direct input on the movie, solidifies two crucial story-telling concepts as a compatible whole; martial arts bullshit and comic book bullshit are 100% compatible and serve as a perfect delivery system for the politically correct bullshit which is at the core of the politically correct America identity, which is steeped in mountains of steaming bullshit.

The orthodoxy of the Great American Lie is paraded as history in the background [Currently, many people get their history from the lead-in back story to such movies, and log the point before the fantastical divergence as actual fact.]to this admitted fantasy, when it is stated that European settlers arrived with their slaves—as if they sailed to Africa, captured some and brought them along—as white pilgrims and black property are shown in still, having just arrived on the coast. In reality it was white human property that was brought along with the first purveyors of our now vast lie, cleared the land, built the plantations and worked them for a hundred and more years before being replaced by more obedient blacks.

Confederate plantations make for good vampire coven settings and are an ideal metaphor for the equally horrible facts. However, rather than continue truthfully with the displacement of the obsolete evil of American chattel slavery with a vastly more effective and all-encompassing evil slave matrix represented by Lincoln and a parade of lesser presidents, Seth reaches into stock, conservative, jingoistic American imagery for a far more pleasing and culturally supportable illusion. In between images of Lincoln butchering the all-white vampires with an axe, we see the Gettysburg Address in vivid color. Seth knows and has mastered the key to commercially successful writing: the subversion of the Ugly Truth with the Beautiful Lie.

I once red Seth's novel on Barabas, as a roguish figure that ultimately saves baby Jesus. Abraham Lincoln Vampire Hunter is no accident. In both stories Seth quotes the bible insightfully and delivers some very fine scenic imagery and bestows outstanding dialogue on his characters. His action is straight out of Hollywood over the top bullshit, with the final package appealing to the young man who normally reads comics.

Who better to sell the lie of universal white privilege and black martyrdom to, than the young paleface nerd wondering why the world hates him yet somehow seeks to appeal to him?

Where the real Abraham Lincoln won a court case consigning a black man to slavery and stated that blacks were inferior and should be shipped back to Africa, Seth's Lincoln is Martin Luther King in white face and top hat. However, the story is appealing even with the obligatory sainted black side kick and the obligatory white devil—who, though a genius always miscalculates. I enjoyed this douchebag movie, I am afraid to admit. But I did and do.

If you are looking into a career writing to sell, I suggest reading Seth Grahame-Smith, whatever he has written, because the guy is a master at wielding the written word as an edifying suspension of disbelief as well as the cultivation of false belief. He should be speech writer to our Mighty Queen when her Wings of State spread and her ghastly Talons of Power rend the throat of our conflicted ancestry to be replaced by a Glittering Lie of Guilt-Gilt White.

Most importantly, not only does Abraham Lincoln Vampire Slayer deliver the message that being born white means that you are among the only race cursed with original sin and it is your duty to protect the innocent races from the natural evil within your foul brood, but the black viewer is schooled, once again, that even though he is a sainted martyr, he's not getting far without a well-spoken white man— preferably a lawyer—to do the heavy lifting for him. As with all such propaganda, the moral taint of being born white and obligated to serve black interests, is balanced by the fact that blacks are born without agency and must look to the White Daddy for deliverance. No message better suits the invaluable maintenance of a multi-racial society as a polity both riven by hatred and shackled by complaisance.

White Master glares down upon us all, not believing anything we believe, or anything he says—the stronger for it.

# 'All Martial Arts Were Stolen from Blacks?'
## 'And Chinese Were Really Black People?': Confucius, Please Say It's Not So!

© 2016 James LaFond

"A FMA grandmaster posted in a forum that all martial arts were stolen from blacks and that the first Chinese were really black people. I ripped him a new one over that so I may be persona non grata in traditional circles now. FMA like everything else is relying on popularity to be successful so they seem as susceptible as any other movement to being pozzed."

-Dave

First, Dave, Has this FMA grandmaster viewed this video?

***Sorry Bro***

If not, you might wish to enlighten him as to the general level of esteem in which our favorite type of American is held in China.

Secondly, let me give you what I know of martial arts evolution—setting aside the very martial art of skewering enemies with weapons and only considering ritualized forms of combat that focus on purposes below the military horizon, such as self-improvement, sports competition, and self-defense, stressing empty hand over weapon use.

Wrestling: Spain, 20,000 Y.B.P.

Boxing: Babylon, 3,700 Y.B.P.

MMA: Hellas, 2,700 Y.B.P.

Some martial arts researchers have attempted to trace the evolution of Chinese martial arts through monastic Indian contact, and have even suggested that the Indians learned it from the Greeks in 327 B.C., as the Ghurkas did, apparently, borrow a Greek sword design, which had been borrowed from an Egyptian pattern. However, a close reading of Alexander's conquests reveals that Indians were already boxing when the God-Brat came on the scene. Below is what I have determined.

The three dates above are more indicative of media advancement than combative advancement.

Warriors wrestle because primitive warriors are hunters and hunters must wrestle game at some point, so wrestling becomes a warrior art.

Boxing is a specific ritual that is closely tied to pastoral nomadism and the battle-taxi chariot, in the period between 2,000 and 1,000 B.C. and was brought to the Near East, Egypt, Indian and the Balkan Peninsula and Adjacent Islands by invading Indo-Europeans. These invaders utilized the same steppes corridor and war technologies that enabled similar barbarians to invade Northern China. I see no reason why Chinese boxing would not also evolve under these same circumstances.

The idea that only one person, in one place, at one time invented, the knife, for instance, or first used a leaf for wiping his ass, or first made a fist and struck with it, and that all subsequent appearances of that practice must be traced linearly back to that source, is an outmoded theory called "diffusion."

31

If one believes that everything in the human tool kit and skill set came about in this manner then an understanding of human behavior and the process of discovery is not likely and will probably not enable that person to process rational discussion.

# When the Shepherd Invites the Wolves to Dinner

### How the Domesticated Humans on One Baltimore Side Street are Adapting to Anarcho-Tyranny

© 2016 James LaFond

This morning I offloaded on Northern Parkway and Glenoak, where I could see four houses for sale that were not for sale last year.

I walk up Glenoak through what is a shallow valley toward the ridgeline a quarter mile off. On the valley floor thee houses are for sale, and four have been recently fitted with security bars.

I Cross the side street connects with Liberty parkway a block over, where a young girl was tortured, raped, killed and burned post mortem by five neighborhood boys a year ago.

As I head up the 40 degree incline to the ridge across which Royston connects Glenoak and Sefton, I see four more for sale signs [all of them vacant], with one under contract and a vacant and one barred house. Just before the corner all but a of the four properties are abandoned.

As I cross Royston, I can look left down into the arm of the valley where the girl was murdered. I look right and see where Royston becomes an unlit, unpaved road. I have found many interesting things among the ground litter at this intersection including vials, cash, needles, pipes... the crows usually choose this vantage to gather in force after sunrise, and they were noisily present today.

I cross Glenmore, the secondary street between Royston Ridge and the Ridge across which White Avenue runs. To my left I see three for sale signs, to my right two.

As I descend into this next depression, the 150 yards of lush city street, supporting single homes and large yards, which one man uses to rebuild Mustangs, I notice two more houses for sale and three barred doors.

The grade uphill to White Avenue is only about 30 degrees and I zigzag over onto Sefton and Mary, where I am surprised to see two older white men discussing their home improvements. The one fellow has fenced his driveway, mounted a flag on his garage and has barred the doors and windows to his large white house with black bars. Dow Mary I see a for sale sign I either direction. Interestingly enough, on this short section of Sefton, which has no addresses on the right, where the man has made his driveway and house into a military compound, older black folks that live there have installed white security bars!

The second man is pointing to the house Charlotte had to give back to the bank as it is being remodeled for sale.

Most of the houses have not sold along this route, but a handful have.

A middle aged black woman walks by toward the bus stop, as to most blacks who live close to Belair Road and the #15 line, but walk twice as far to catch the #19 on Harford Road, which is getting worse, but is nothing like Belair Road. A young black woman dressed in white with bowties in her hair is screaming obscenities into her phone.

As I turn the corner onto White Avenue across from the halfway house, I turn to head toward Harford Road and notice that two houses are for sale in that direction.

Most people just cannot afford to move.

Some people cannot afford to stay.

Others fortify their homes.

Some cannot afford bars on their doors.

The drug war is being waged aggressively, my white neighbors being snatched off the sidewalks by cops and all of the dealers in between Walther and Harford being raided except for Binkie, who must know someone. Cops often roar down White and Glenmore, Harford and Walther, the two primary and two secondary streets that border this grid. At least once a week cops kick in a door. But, never is a cop car on patrol, deterring crime by his presence on the side streets. The police have utterly given up the preventative role and only pursue drug busts and major and answer emergency calls.

The shepherd has opened the gate to the sheep pen and invited the wolves to dine. I am expecting an interesting feast.

## 'They Are a Strawman'
### The Evil Step-Mother of All Conspiracy Theories with Walter Blakely

© 2016 James LaFond

"James,

Re: *The Clarity Of Decline*

"Ask yourself:

"Who controls Hollywood and makes these movies?

"Who sets the agenda to prevent children from learning in school?

"Who guarantees that less than 3% of the population that are perverts can drive the narrative?

"As Marx said, 'Their god is money and their religion is huckstering.'

"I agree [with you] that they are a strawman for the ones that really direct.

"But who is that?"

-Walter Blakely

You know, Walter, six years ago I retired from the worship of the God of Things to retire to the reclusive life of the heretic and try and empty my brain in hopes of outpacing insanity. But lately, I exist in a panicked literary state as I publish book after book this summer, as what I can only call superstition seems to overtake me. With the mental space to read and write and think previously denied me as I slaved for my earthly god, I have come to view the hierarchies which we toil and agonize to serve—most of us believing the fiction that they serve us—as a ranked army of straw men shielding some true puppet master.

As someone who has denied conspiracy theories most of my life as the simpleton solutions of eccentrics with too much mental energy and not enough facts, I now find myself rowing in that very babbling boat!

My readers tend to express the opinion that our masters hide behind the curtain to the left, while most folks seem to believe that our puppet master or masters reside behind the curtain to the right.

I, in my premature dotage, am stricken with the irrational sense that our master is a monstrous being and that he does have two faces he holds forth for the wicked world.

Over the past three years I have been studying myself for signs of decline out of the vainly odd desire to be able to write believably aging characters.

There are three things that happen to me with disturbing regularity, which have been happening since 2006, when I first came under extreme job, relationship and combat [fighting men who were world class, while being manifestly not] stress:

Black "phantoms" usually in the form of streaks of shadow appear, disappear and dart around my visual periphery. Not a lot, a few times a day, usually as I ponder something.

1. Am I going insane?

2. Am I experiencing something extra-material?

3. Is this a medical condition?

Time seems to stop, usually when I am seeing things more clearly than previously, at which point either my hearing temporarily shuts down or things grow silent. I'm inclined to the former. At these times I am overcome by a profound sense that the people and places of my life are nothing more than baffling constructs of an unseen mind—that my every human contact are so vastly improbably that what and who are dear to me, simply could not be.

1. Am I a malfunctioning facet of a video game?

2. Am I going insane on a chemical level?

3. Was Phillip K. Dick God and I his sympathetic doomed character?

4. Are demons attempting to possess me?

5. Am I an alien abduction victim?

6. Did that drug that Ron Bone put in my drink when I was 19 really mess me up and this world of whining manginas, raging cunts and smart phones are all just

a messed up dream, and that instead we have settled the moon and are exploring Mars and launching the Titan satellite station as I vegetate in a coma...

Animals—even the notoriously low IQ hoodrat—seem to be able to sense my intent. For instance, this morning, the new cat that my roommate's insane girl brought into the house to help the older cat patrol for the Harm City Mouseketeers, was hassling me for food. Its human mother is out on a chemical vacation and I do not feed cats, or otherwise slave for any four-leg. The older female cat and young male cat have been getting along famously. Although I ignore the old cat totally, she has always brought kills to me, like I am her god of death, even eating rabbit brains next to me on the porch. Well, as I glared at this big tom cat to bug off, this old bitch cat pounced like my avatar—a picture of venomous fury—and had the big tom cowering in the corner. The other morning, walking home, I could swear the crows at the top of Royston were hopping along next to me, keeping me in sight.

I am now superstitious.

Maybe it is an accumulation of almost 30 concussions and 20 years of extreme sleep deprivation?

But the cold chill down my spine while I wrote this makes me want to believe—nay feel—that I have just awakened in the chamber where we all spin on our meat-sticks, feeding some furnace-like mind.

Rationally, speaking, from my admittedly cracked perspective, Walter, a small group like the gays, the Albanians, or the bankers of Brussels—or if you want to get really fanciful, some dysfunctional tribe out of the ancient world that has only managed to survive by scattering to do those things guaranteed to make them hated and persecuted—must have a backer, must, like Jameel McCrack Deal, have a Tyronator to back him up when the crack-heads decide they want their fix for free.

Who is, we muse, the Global Tyronator?

Part of me wants to find out. The other part of me doesn't want to see what is attached to those phantom feet behind the curtains that hem us blindly in.

# The First Wave
### Dindu Annexation Tactical Phases

© 2016 James LaFond

Currently the four Baltimore County police precincts I am keeping up on are in various stages of Dindu annexation. You will note that outlying suburbs are targeted by the government for Dinduization based on income.

The White Marsh precinct is broken into two zones, Inner and Outer.

Geography notes, from East to West: Essex is against the water, a coastal plain, with White Marsh being mixed wetlands and ridges, Parkville low hills, and Towson a valley nestled between the low hills of Parkville and the piedmont proper, to the west, north and northwest, with such areas as Upperco, Cockeysville, and Westminster. One may drive north from Towson along a rising ridgeline into the Lancaster area of Southern Pennsylvania.

## Phase 1: Towson

*Upper Middle Class to Affluent*

Towson is the County Seat, where multiculturalism is embraced, with medical facilities and universities hosting many Dindus, who typically attack pedestrians in public places as a form of cultural angst expression and are largely excused by the elite.

## Phase 2: Outer White Marsh

*Upper Middle Class*

Large commercial centers staffed by numerous honest Dindus provide cover for Dindu pedestrians, resulting in the highest incidence of muggings and armed robberies. The large Avenue Theater hosts thousands of urban Dindus per day, resulting in numerous beatings of palefaces. Burglary is on the rise.

**Phase 3: Parkville**

*Working to Middle Class*

Available failed mortgages and apartment complexes have been the target of resettlement from City projects, resulting in the expansion of the Dindu population from 8-255 in one year, and the complete takeover of local schools by Dindu gangs. Parkville Senior High was the scene of fur mob attacks—within sight of the Parkville Police Precinct—with police and media obscuring and denying the school and racial nature of the crimes. Though the population is lightly less than 25% Dindu, people seen on the street are 80% Dindu.

They key component here is double to quadruple Dindu visibility and crime, along with misreporting and obfuscation of crime trends by the media.

-Honest Dindus have been extensively targeted by Dindu criminals.

-Convenience stores are robbed weekly, the police taking no preventative measures and making little effort to capture the bandits.

-Men walk the street at night in pairs, breaking into vehicles.

-Young men molest teen girls on the street.

-Honest Dindus who move in bar their doors.

-Mobs of Dindus attack lone Dindus.

-Middle-aged Dindus drink on street corners until five a.m.

-Winos now congregate in children's parks during the day.

-Burglaries are skyrocketing and bars are going up on windows

## Phase 4: Inner White Marsh

*Working Class*

Inner White Marsh is really Rosedale, which borders the city and straddles the Parkville and White Marsh precinct lines and is ignored by officers from both stations. It is the same as Parkville, except that whites are now targeted on sight at night and increasingly by day by mobs of Dindu youth. Also, pairs of adult Dindus strike out on long range patrols from the city, committing walk-through crimes and then spending the morning with relatives in Essex or White Marsh. When law enforcement personnel are known to be busy elsewhere, car loads of Dindu men cruise, looking for lone Palefaces to beat, brick and club.

**Phase 5: Essex**

*Working Class*

Essex, first targeted in the early 1990s, is now distinguishable from City ghettos only in terms of sprawl. Palefaces on foot at night are relentlessly hunted by Dindu mobs, adult teams and lone actors. Professional Dindu criminals are now kicking in Dindu doors and establishing a reign of terror identical to that found in the West Baltimore and East Baltimore Dindu enclaves they were bussed in from— more from the Westside than the Eastside, for the affluent, northerly County Seat of Towson and the affluent Jewish enclaves of Western Baltimore County are not willing to absorb the Dindu invaders and have [through business and government action] directed their migration to hit the working class Eastern County.

Four bus lines designed to move Dindus deeper into the County and up into affluent Harford County, have just been established.

Welcome to Dindustan—it's coming to you!

## Parting the Curtain of the Lie
**Walking on the Corpse of a City in the Wake of the Ascension of Freddie Gray: Part 1 of 5**

© 2016 James LaFond

Megan is a woman I have known for ten years, much more of a Baltimorean than I, a girl who grew up in East and Northeast Baltimore with the system, luck and gender against her. She was being beaten and attacked by white men back when cops laughed at such crimes. Now, at the other end of a topsy-turvy life, she works at a "financial center" in Hamilton, being threatened and stalked by Dindus daily, in an age when all Dindus are saints and martyrs and no sensible cop will raise a hand to them.

Megan has gotten by on heart and character her entire life, which makes her heart ailment especially troubling. Last year, after knocking on her Cedonia door to see if she and her roommates [women, children and a disabled guy] were okay, I had four Warrior Martyrs of the Lie chasing me down the street, their leader calling for weapons as they closed in.

Megan is now moving to the tip of a wind-kissed suburban Peninsula, four miles from the closest extended bus line, in a bypassed enclave, off the Dindustan map. Her daughter and infant grandchild are now teaming up with her to make a go at life in a manless society—for daddy is a Dinduized paleface who believes work is for women and chumps.

There remains the problem of income. Megan makes her living in Hamilton and her daughter works one block from the Media Riot Zone. They must both manage a daily or nightly escape from Dindustan. When Megan asked me to help her move, I was expecting to haul her few bags of clothes.

The financial center closes at 4 p.m., before dark in winter, when the Dindu hunters rise from their Dindu dens. Her daughter would be available to pick her up at seven. That leaves Megan in Dindustan for three hours. She had already transported her clothes and needed me to walk her to the dollar store so she could buy baby clothes, pillows, sheets and various things for the tiny person she calls "Tweet."

This woman knows Hamilton, and knows well that she can't walk these streets without an escort. She was also motivated by a morbid curiosity to see firsthand, on foot, what became of her girlhood homeland. There was also advice she was seeking, wondering what ideas I might have for evacuation methods when The Paleface Purge heats up again: what she should do in a snow storm, the safest way out of the city for her daughter in periods of unrest, what streets should be used to get from Hamilton to the interstate when her daughter shuttles her to and from work. Much of this will hopefully be applied to her use of a car as soon as she can purchase one.

Then there was the matter of family heritage. Would I be willing, maybe one Saturday a month, to escort her and her granddaughter to see her grandmother's old store, her family's ancient, Catholic church, the Aquarium, the Science Center and Fort McHenry at the Inner Harbor—to get an ice cream cone or snowball without fear that she wouldn't be able to protect her Tweet? Her life is one of daily death-threats and beating threats by younger, larger more numerous males and females of the Dindu kind. For a person for whom sex would be a coronary death sentence, the prospect of fighting off men and beast women with her fists, as she did in her youth, is terrifying.

My answer was, of course, yes. I trust her to sit down and curl up in a corner with the baby and then give an exonerating report to the pigs when they swoop in, in their Dindu support role, hopefully keeping me out of their clutches.

What follows is a ridiculous amount of Harm City material, collected over the course of a half mile stroll on a sunny, breeze-cooled, Saturday afternoon, followed by a brief chat over a sipped shot of whiskey in my room, in front of this godlike typewriter. But first, there is the ascension of the city's patron saint to consider...

The first three of the six cops to be tried for the crucifixion of Freddie "Jesus" Gray do not reside behind bars. Indeed, the presiding judge [black] has castigated the prosecution, ripping their case apart. The lead detective for the prosecution [black] wrote notes last year indicating that she felt compelled to relate a patently false "narrative" to the grand jury.

53

The police officers are preparing to launch law suits for slander, etc.

On White Avenue, Palefaces quietly whisper about the case, becoming hushed as I walk by.

Blacks loudly argue the case, becoming louder as I walk by, shouting their arguments from five feet apart.

Every time another negative report concerning Baltimore City's crusade to lynch three blacks and three whites for the death of one Dindu drug dealer, Megan has customers come to her window and threaten her with violence for the color of her skin, even as she provides their financial service and wishes them a good day.

Half of the hackers [older black men] who have provided her with transportation, have been robbed at gunpoint by young Dindu Warriors.

One of the [black] security guards, whose job it was to protect her, was executed by three masked men only a few weeks back.

She does not want to work in Baltimore, but she is aging, white and in bad health, putting her at the bottom of most hiring agendas.

Even when she gets a car, merely visiting her mother's grave will be dangerous.

Her surviving brother's daughters have chosen to be impregnated by Dindustani men, who they insist on bringing to family gatherings, even though these men steal the cash, medication and other contents of the older aunts' purses while they are preparing the meal for these predatory cross-breeders. In the face of this she plans an isolated nuclear family life in their waterfront haven away from a toxifying extended family.

The young men in her extended family are all drug addicts.

Her ability to acquire male protection is limited to paying elderly black men a small fee to see her to her front door—a task that has claimed half of them in the name of the Hip Hop degeneration—and to call up a never-was boxer for a walk to the store.

# Dawn in Dindustan

I received the call at 4:10 p.m., as she stood on my land lord's porch, having hired a ride to bring her. I could have walked down into Hamilton and walked her up the hill, but uphill walks under the summer sun are too much for her heart. We will stroll along the ridge line, a quarter-mile wide along Harford Road.

What follows is a middle-aged, urban, paleface, pedestrian saga, that lasted from 4:20-6:38 p.m., on a sunny Saturday evening, at the End of Civilized Time.

# Little Book Girl
## Walking on the Corpse of a City in the Wake of the Ascension of Freddie Gray: Part 2 of 5

© 2016 James LaFond

As we walked out White Avenue she spoke whimsically of Mary Avenue, the third of the five parallel streets that travel east to west across this ridgeline. I told her it was not safe to walk on by day anymore, as the apartment complex three blocks to our rear and north was now infested with section eights and vacancies were sprouting up alongside for sale signs, foreclosure signs and steel door and window bars. Half of the foot traffic on Mary is juvenile and drug deals are conducted in the middle of the street from double-parked SUVs.

We walked past the last house on the right, which she noted, "...belongs in a country orchard, not here."

I noted that this had once been a country orchard.

We walked through the church parking lot, across the overgrown alley—a thicket hunted by alley cats and foxes—and across the Harbel Community Center [which supports the influx of drug addicts into the neighborhood] parking lot, to Mary Avenue, behind the former expanse of the Peter G. Angelos law firm, which grew rich on Mesothelioma suits against asbestos manufacturers on behalf of shipyard workers, and permitted the lawyer a seat on the Baltimore Orioles Ownership Board.

Crossing the not very busy mainstreet of Harford Road, is a ten year old blonde girl, in a dress, with a purse and a little on the heavy side, looking nervously about as she cradles the book she seems to treasure against her purse, obviously coming from the library across the street that is barely out of sight. As she crosses and begins walking down Mary, Megan groans and mutters, "Whoever her drug addicted bitch mother is should be hung up by her twat for letting this child walk these streets."

The girl glances at us and looks nervously behind her, and we see him there. There is a Dindu boy of about 12 that was walking out Harford Road, who looked at her, looked around, looked at us, looked at her and then changed directions to follow the girl.

Megan said, "We're not letting this happen and stepped up on the far corner and turned to watch the pursuit. She knows me well enough to know that I would normally—as a Darwinist who sees no sense in saving a dying blood line—let the blooming crime develop rather than risk martyring the Dindu boy-saint and ruining what is left of my life as the next George Zimmerman. She also knows that I'm subject to her moral approval and is using me to do a good deed. We stand and watch as the pursuit develops, my gauging the distance and relative food speed. I'm still fast in a sprint up to 100 meters. This punk is between us and my second floor armory, and if I touch him, I'll be fighting members of his gang set [they show up in the next part] along with uncles and cousins and at least one big fat MaBabayDinduShit bitch in a probably unsuccessful bid to get Megan home. But she cares less about herself than this girl—wedded to motherhood and outmoded notions of right and wrong as she is.

More Dindus mill about further down Mary.

Megan stands next to me whispering to herself, "Please, Little Girl, don't go down Mary."

The girl cut into the Harbel back lot in the direction we came from, toward White, and Megan growled, "Good Girl—your mom might be a dumb bitch. But it doesn't mean you have to be."

The Dindu boy then looks at the girl and stops. He begins to follow her and then looks over his shoulder at us, seemingly undecided. Megan snarls under her breath, "Keep going, Coon!"

The boy resumes walking down Mary, takes three steps, stops, looks at the girl as she glances fearfully over her shoulder at him, clutching her story book [It looked like a Golden Book], picking up her pace. It is as if she is in an adolescent never-never land where parents never reach into to aid a child, as she never glances at us for help or consideration, and seems totally alone in the world in her mind.

The Dindu boy looks at us again and Megan shudders as she clenches her fists and snarls, "Keep going, Coon!"

The boy then looks specifically at me, looks back at the girl, who is now out of our sight behind the building, and looks back at me as I step toward him so that I can get the girl back in my sight. He then gawks open eyed, turns on his heels and walks down Mary as if nothing had ever passed between us.

As we walk on, Megan rants and raves in muttering tones about coons, drug-addict white bitches and slacker vagina faggots, until we hit Harford Road and the smell of Restive Dindustan hits us.

# Dindustani Customer Service
### Walking on the Corpse of a City in the Wake of the Ascension of Freddie Gray: Part 3 of 5

© 2016 James LaFond

The street is nearly deserted. The library across the street is boarded up, the windows kicked in again, but still in business. We are on the sidewalk where Peter G. Angelos' proud building has just been smashed into, looted of whatever remains, and burned by the Mary Avenue Set, who name themselves according to four letters, two of which are either Zs or Ss. I cannot decipher their tag.

These boys have been busy establishing their reign through random acts of terror these past six months. I ran into three of them fifty yards from this spot last Monday morning at 4 a.m. They have taken half of the territory that belonged to the Liberty Parkway Boyz who raped and killed a girl last year and got busted. A half mile out Harford, at the bottom of the ridge, is a professional gang of teens who are openly tolerated by the police and who cut multiple kilos of dope up on a basement table beneath the hair salon they hang out in front of. I have witnessed narc cops taking down suspected white customers, but they leave the Valentino Crew alone. We stand in a zone between set ranges, savoring the smell of this vacant building, its shell rescued by the fire department—fenced now, no longer providing shelter for Mister Africa or Lice Man on a rainy day.

We run into Reba and Tom, two Oxy pill poppers, with their three-year-old boy, who still does not talk and never has a toy to play with, and is fed candy by Reba. Reba asks Megan for some money for food for the baby and Megan glares at Tom, "Not while you're with that piece of shit."

Tom, a tall, handsome, athletic guy in his mid-twenties, whined, "That's not fair, Miss Megan. I'm working."

"Yeah, and how much money have you spent on food for the baby?"

Silence as the junky head drops.

63

The baby is standing next to his former stroller, which now packs mom's purse, looking dumbly about. Megan smiles at him, gives the baby hand wave and says to Tom, "Have you bought him a toy yet, anything? Or is he still playing with the wipe box container?"

"Come on Miss Megan, work is hard on me. I have a bad back."

"Yeah," she snarls, and you'll be on it in a week, living off of Reba. If you were my son in law, I'd stuff a sock in your mouth so you never woke up and paint a sign on your pretty face, 'here lies the vagina of the house!'"

Reba then led her boy and her drone away as Megan shook her head and said, "Buy him some grapes at least—instead of Skittles!"

I walked Megan to the 7-11, and we stopped to let a redneck in a giant pickup make his turn. He would have normally shook his head at me, a white man on foot, gone Dindu, but he waved, as Megan smiled at him and waved him on around the corner.

As Megan went into the 7-11 I walked across to the Ibis, West Indian bar to get a half pint of whiskey. One drunken white man sat drooling and twitching at the bar. A Jamaican girl and another West Indian—a man—were discussing something and ignored me as a I stood at the bar for five minutes, so I left.

The Shamrock, the stoner bar, had one white man tittering dazedly outside, trying to light his cigarette. Inside, with no patrons, the owner slept on the bar top—big, Neanderthal-Aryan and heavy browed, snoring away.

I crossed the street to greet Megan as she emerged from the 7-11, angry over the rude African man who did not want to wait on her.

On we went, to the dollar store.

# 'The Police Have Been Notified'
### Walking on the Corpse of a City in the Wake of the Ascension of Freddie Gray: Part 4 of 5

© 2016 James LaFond

We walked past the garage, where there was no staff present. The alarm was going off, announcing to those who had broken in the side of the building that the police were on their way, and that they should exit.

We continued on by and halted, as two large, well-dressed and helmeted, upscale Dindu warriors zoomed around in the center of the street, describing a U-turn on their high-powered Japanese racing bikes and then rode up onto the curb in front of us. They dismounted as we stood back. They then entered the barber shop and took a seat as we walked by and I gawked at the large photo of Ali standing over Sonny Liston posted in the window.

In the middle of the intersection of Christopher and Harford, four Harley Davidsons rumbled. When we turned to look we did not see Dante and the Chosen Sons but three older black bikers, with German-style black helmets and leathers on, escorting a very large female of the silver-backed kind, who was attempting to learn how to driver her Harley, which was wheezing audibly. Megan said, "Those men should take that dumb bitch to a parking lot before her fat ass decorated the grill of a city bus. She said this as the #19 to Carney zoomed by the crawling bikers.

We turned the corner to the remodeled dollar store, passed a blonde junky who was doing the 90 degree dopefiend lean and dug into her big purse absently. I held the door for Megan to enter, and then headed downhill, out Harford Road to the Sikh Liquor Store, right on the edge of Valentino Boy territory. I did not go as far as the bus stop which is no longer used at night, but only covered two of the five remaining blocks, past Anthony Goh's now relocated World Wushu Federation American Headquarters [now, like most storefronts, a Dindu beauty salon] and entered the extremely well stocked and merchandized liquor store, staffed against robbery by three.

The owners son—a tall, young man in traditional indigo turban—stood back behind the register until I took my sunglasses off. The register is on a raised platform. Next to him is his meat shield, the guy who puts stuff in a bag and will soak up lead when the Dindus come in. The owner's son keeps a hand gun on a shelf under the register, not removing his hand until I walk past their flanker and state my business. I want a half pint of Makers Mark.

In order to step up to the counter I had to pass the tall man in T-shirt and jeans—who seems nervous—and has a folding knife in the palm of his half-pocketed right hand.

As I make my purchase they all three wish me a good day, and then organize against the next potential gunman, the large Dindu with the beard, looking at rum and vodka on the discount rack.

Outside I pass two Valentino Set members who have just escorted a muscular dirt bag and his slutty girlfriend—two white trash dopers—to the extremity of their range. She was fussing with her bunched up shorts and flip flops and he was smacking his grimy fist into his palm, an extremely muscular, gravelly voiced blonde man with a skin-scorching tan, in wife beater and jeans.

Up the hill I go with my wax-sealed bottle of spirits.

# Derrick's Indigo Tear
## Walking on the Corpse of a City in the Wake of the Ascension of Freddie Gray: Part 5 of 5

© 2016 James LaFond

I entered the dollar store to the greeting of "Welcome, Sir," from the tall, muscular, light-skinned, gang-tattooed cashier at the first lane. There was a vastly-hipped pear-shaped woman running the front end, and a not very bright young man of the same age and condition, but with beard and darker compaction. The three staff were only outnumbered by the customers by 1. There was Megan, pushing pillows and baby clothes in a small cart.

There was a lady leaving with her purchase.

Before me, as I walked in, was a dark-skinned woman a wearing shear purple poncho, which did not conceal her enormous breasts. She was perhaps six and a half feet tall in heels, and broke into a wide smile when she greeted me with a "Hello, babay."

I politely tipped my hat as I returned the smile and wondered if each of her breasts were indeed larger than my head. She certainly suffered from an unresolved, white-daddy fantasy abetted by a Santa Clause fetish. As I walked over to Megan, the woman's bright smile inverted into a dark grin and she glared at Megan, who pushed her cart down the aisle hurriedly, whispering, "Good Lord, that beast woman wants you. Christ, she could be the wet nurse for the Washington Redskins!"

I followed Megan around as she pretended to shop, glancing over the aisle tops, until she saw the towering shadow of a woman leave by the front door, and determined it was safe to come up front and purchase medicine, chiding me under her breath, "Oh, not much has changed. The monster bitches still love dey Mista Jimmay."

Our checkout ordeal was mildly comical, as these three former gang members, trying to start life afresh at minimum wage in their late twenties, stumbled good naturedly through the process that we both used to supervise a full decade ago.

The vastly hipped woman glanced jealously at Megan as I tried to figure out how much her ass actually weighed—I think more than Derrick—who was our cashier. Derrick was such a fine looking athletic specimen that I almost asked him if he'd be interested in boxing.

Derrick was tan to goldenrod in complexion and had an impressive collection of tattoos:

1. A Crown Royal bottle on his right neck, from collar bone to ear

2. A heart-shaped tear under his left eye

3. The name, birth date and date of death of a friend, tattooed over an RIP on his left neck

4. Another RIP notice on his left arm

5. Two names in Arabic tattooed down his right arm

6. Various tattoos on his hands and the back of his arms which I could not make out

Derrick was as nervous handling Megan's purchases and money as the two Middle-Eastern guys who were helping the Sikh liquor store owner's son, guard his property. Derrick and his coworker were trying very hard to be something they do not appear to have been for long. Megan and I complimented them on their efforts—able to tell after training hundreds such clerks, that they really were trying to learn their new occupation. Cobbling together a work force from such broken people is no easy thing.

The walk home was uneventful, and the chat over whiskey is where I got the back story for this little shopping expedition that appears in part one of this series. I do not have a certain overall opinion or thought concerning this insightful stroll through a neighborhood under attack by Dindu horde, only that this dead place appears—to me at least—to be its own goal.

## 'An Outpost of Civilization'
### A Case for Culture and Cult when 'Government/Media/All Right-Thinking Citizens are Against You'

© 2016 B & James LaFond

*Below is a rebuttal of my piece **Holding Out** which I liked very much. B is correct in his analysis of my proposal. The fact is, without a culture, which we have been denied, most humans are not going to hold out beyond the individual level and that is not a level that most humans are comfortable with. Much of my advice is for that odd man out who is comfortable with being the outsider on the inside. Consider that the United States is directly evolved out of a mercantile model that had two purposes:*

1. The destruction of native culture

2. The exploitation of the lower classes, as inferior beings that do not share the same culture as the upper classes, culture according to gross accumulation, denial of culture via impoverishment.

*How could any polity evolved out of this purpose not behave in terms of hierarchal predation and cultural eradication? My article Holding Out was essentially methodology for Lost Cause resistance based on my coming of age as a loner in a cultureless society. If you think we had a Christian society in the 1960s and 70s, you are mistaken. It was nominally Christian. Now, to identify yourself as Christian is an odd form of self-limiting labeling in the face of the atheistic State. The problem with Christianity as a cross-cultural evangelical force is that when culture becomes divorced from faith, the faith is then dissolved by extra-cultural means. B is a practicing Jew, not the parttime, secularized Jews we have grown used to, which means he is a member of an intact culture, where I have never been the member of an intact culture. Also, his occupational background is special operations military, from a unit type involved with operational impact on society, where I am just an urban survivor, so his perspective is the opposite of mine on macro and micro levels and therefore offers an appropriate perspective for a counterpoint.*

James,

Glad you adapted "dindu"-it's a great term.

I disagree with the post [Holding Out]. Here's why:

The question is, how do you carve out an outpost of civilization and a functional community in the modern city environment, given that the government/media/all right-thinking citizens are against you.

You have a method that sort of worked for you in the absence of a community/support (one man is an island, sometimes,) and your reasoning is to scale that method up. You conclude that it's unworkable. This is sort of like a guy who is an expert survivalist and can knap knives out of obsidian being asked how it can be arranged for everyone to have all the knives they need. He thinks about how much time it would take to teach everyone to knap knives, how much of a pain in the ass obsidian is to find, how often a knife made of obsidian needs re-knapping, and concludes that the process is not scalable.

Well, right-to solve this problem at scale, you need very different tools, and the knives will be different. An automated knife factory making 10K knives a month looks nothing like 1000 master obsidian knife makers.

The way for whiteys to solve this problem at scale, I think, is by looking at communities which have solved it. The only two I know are Jewish neighborhoods in New York, Williamsburg and Crown Heights (Irish/Italian working class neighborhoods improvised a stopgap solution, which is failing slowly as the kids leave or become niggerized). I will discuss in detail below.

Summary: from the 1930s onwards, the State waged war by proxy against ethnic white communities, including Jewish ones, in American cities. They would forcibly integrate blacks, who would ethnically cleanse those communities. NYC went from being a third Jewish to something like 10%. Two Jewish communities remain in areas which are full of blacks, Crown Heights and Williamsburg. Both started off mixed, with many different kinds of Jews, and are now homogeneous. Both are Hasidic, Crown Heights Jews being Chabad Hasidim and Williamsburg Jews being Satmar Hasidim. I'm better acquainted with Crown Heights, so will mostly discuss it.

Background: in the 1960s and 70s, blacks were moved into both neighborhoods. All whites fled due to crime and associated falling home values. The police refused to do their job except when it came to targeting lawabiding citizens engaging in self defence, and the city disarmed those citizens (the history is quite illuminating.) http://nypost.com/2012/01/16/the-strange-birth-of-nys-gun-laws/

The fight back: The rebbes (leaders) of Chabad and Satmar announced to their Hasidim (followers) that they would not be going anywhere. To the extent that they could, they bought up the houses and synagogues that those fleeing left behind. In both neighborhoods, Jews were subject to TNB (robbery, rape, murder.) They responded in two ways. First, by forming official neighborhood patrols that cooperated with police, wore uniforms, etc. Second, young men worked informally; a friend of mine tells me that when he and his friends walked down the street in Crown Heights in the 1970s and they would encounter a black teenager or two, they would beat them up with no questions asked. Additionally, Satmar in

Williamsburg has something called "hopsin" (which means "get him" in Yiddish, I think): when someone is attacked/robbed, he yells "hopsin!" and everyone in earshot yells it as well and runs to grab the criminal and hold him for the police.

All this culminated in the mass looting of the New York City Blackout of 1977 and then the Crown Heights Riot, the latter encouraged by the Mayor of NYC and the New York Times, with the NYPD standing by. In the latter, the Jews fought back to some extent, hampered by the lack of guns (if they had guns, they would have defended themselves like the Koreans of the LA riots.) A bus of Satmar Hasidim with bats was sent to help by the Satmar rebbe (typically, Satmar and Chabad really disliked each other.)

For the last 20 years, things have been quiet. The blacks have calmed way down, as they realized that ethnically cleansing the Jews is not in the cards (of course, sporadic crime continues.) Hipsters have been gentrifying both neighborhoods since the mid-2000s.

Lessons learned: a community can't stick together against dindus and their sponsors/masters based on ethnicity or even religion alone. It needs to be cultish, with a single strong and charismatic leader with a vision. It also helps uniforms worn by all the members, to make identification difficult ("which one stabbed you?" "Uh, he had a beard, black pants, white shirt.") It's forbidden for Jews to turn one another over to the cops, and if you go to jail, you know the community will support your family. The weird/crazy aspect that Hasidic Jews present to the typical Irish/Italian/black cop helps mitigate law enforcement anarchotyranny. You also need to be able to vote as a block, make appropriate campaign contributions and lawyer up (and contribute to legal defense and political lobbying for members who get balled up by cops.) You need to have a large fraction of your males working in businesses in the community during the day, to hold ground, to have justification to move dindus along from in front of the business, and to have a constant reserve of members in the area. You need your own educational institutions, also in the community, not public schools where your kids will be victimized. Those of your educational institutions where teenagers and young men study provide another reserve of available manpower against packs of dindus. You really, really need a religious code that commands deep loyalty within the group and self-sufficient values (an NYT article holds no weight with Hasidim, for instance) as well as deep cynicism about outsiders and their motivations.

In short, none of this will work without a deep and crazy belief in G-d (in an everyday way, not in a Universalist overarching way) and community leadership, and structures built on the above.

Thoughts?

Sincerely,

B

**James' Thoughts**

Uniform dress and grooming style, if not uniforms [which can be legislated against, like the Guardian Angels being prohibited in Baltimore County] is an excellent idea and should be used by any resistance group. The Dindu raiders do it with much success: white T, black cargo shorts, bald head, sneakers.

On a practical level, holding ground through buying real estate and operating businesses is key to community resistance in a purely materialistic society. For example, when I have had to defend myself and family on property I was buying or renting the cops supported the criminal attackers. Consider that home buyers are not really owners and that even if you own your home the sidewalk is usually public property and your yard—in many municipalities—is not regarded as your home, but as a buffer you are supposed to retreat from as you grovel inside of your home while your car, bike, family pet or son are torn apart by Dindu raiders outside.

Now, as a business operator, managing a retail outlet for the owners, I was essentially a law enforcement auxiliary. I could not get away with the actions that cops did, but they backed me up as long as I minimized my use of force. A business that size anchors a neighborhood in terms of real estate taxes, operating taxes and sales taxes and is a priority concern for the State. If a homeowner leaves because of crime, the bank still has to pay the taxes and will sell it to another owner eventually. It's not good for the municipal parasitic apparatus, but not a disaster. Now, when a business closes the property owner can write it off as a loss, reducing tax income for the municipality and more importantly, eliminates sales taxes, container taxes, tobacco taxes, alcohol taxes, egg handling taxes [I shit you not], food handling taxes [licensing fees], unemployment taxes [whatever your employer pays you, a percentage gets sent to the government], matching SSI taxes and inventory taxes! Also, the merchant can make a legal case for patrolling the sidewalk in order to facilitate the safe entry and exit of patrons, where a home owner has little ground to stand on when it comes to keeping the sidewalk in front of his house safe.

Based on the manner in which breakaway Christian denominations are labeled cults by the media and the extra attention paid to any Christian cult by the American State, I think that the generation of such a community in the face of the greater society's wishes, will be difficult to pull off. I see the efforts of those trying to construct tribal identities from scratch facing Federal persecution at the point where the Dindu hordes meet resistance.

With that said, without a cultic component, there is no hope of organized community resistance. Those beliefs that are in particular weak in the face of the irrational, race-based attacks are libertarian types who have only rationality.

In retrospect, my weird life and my ability to go it alone, while enabled in large measure by my rational diplomatic ability, has, in times of crises, only been salvaged by an odd faith in my racial heritage. Two of my Uncles, my maternal grandfather, and heavy doses of 1920s-30s adventure, fantasy and science fiction novels read as a boy, as well as many imperialistic movies viewed with my father and grandfather, somehow resulted in my firmest belief, which I have taken to be my inherited identity: that it is the plight of a handful of men of European origin to have souls— where most of humanity utterly lacks a transcendental element—and that this fact translates into a savage plight, that a few white men will always find it necessary to dominate and strive against massed subhuman hordes or perish. This is why I have always been against breeding a lot of whites in a materialistic setting, as it turns our race into subhumans.

Now, this is a nutty notion, developed largely under the influence of childhood bullies and fictional literary refuge, while in contact with men who prevailed in WWII and Korea. Yet, when black men came to my house to take my son away, when black men pulled guns on me, when they rushed me in mob strength, set their pit bulls on me, hurled stones at me, it was exactly this nutty—most would say insane—notion that was the basis for my survival and in most cases, dominance.

How do we—as humans in a subhuman world—scale that up?

Cultic, culturally identified, metaphysics.

I get it.

I agree.

And I step aside to live out the remainder of my own weird life, only concerned with helping those with whom I can identify—alienated humans who find themselves on the heaving seas of subhuman insanity.

I certainly would not advise them against forming a cult, but am not equipped to help, simply inclined to wish them well.


**Addendum**

Aside from the Arabs, of course, we [Israel] have a ton of Eritrean and Sudanese illegal immigrants. These guys walked across Egypt and got smuggled across the Sinai to get here. The government settled them in South Tel Aviv, which was a lower-class Jewish neighborhood (kind of like working class white places in Philly/Baltimore/NYC.) They've made it unlivable, with theft, assault, rape, trash, etc. Of course, the leftists are on their side-they're "refugees," you can't deport them, etc.

Here's Haaretz, our New York Times, writing about May Golan, a Jewish girl who has been attempting to organize to do something about them: http://www.haaretz.com/israel-news/.premium-1.570191

Here's Latma, a pretty funny Israeli satirical show, on the subject: https://youtu.be/QcjSe_GTVXA

Political correctness has not really taken off well here, fortunately.

Sincerely,

B

# Killers Matter
## The People's Republic of Maryland takes Steps to Further Endanger its Tax Slaves

© 2016 James LaFond

The most violent and unreachable murderers will soon be granted work release and loosened parole restrictions. The story in Maryland goes, when a 14-year-old boy steals a vehicle, maims and cripples a crossing guard, and kills an 8-year-old girl, that "two lives have been ruined." This is how the Dindu leadership see such a crime. The carjacker was innocent, simply acting out without agency as a zombie, according to the root causation [long dead white men] and his resulting light juvenile sentence is considered a heinous crime against Dindukind becaseu it will hurt his job opportunities. He is already a full blown idiot pshychopath, but spending a few years in a facility is more wrong than the older black woman who will be crippled for life and on par with the young innocent life he snuffed out.

In that same vein, amid cheering criminals gathered in the streets of the city they are destroying, The Evil State of Maryland has announced that youths who have commited the most wicked crimes that called for trial as an adult [unlike the above-mentioned carjacker who will be tried as a juvenile] like the gang rape, torture and immolation of my neighbor, will be given every chance to get back into striking position to do the bidding of their masters—terrorizing tax payers.

Welcome to Dindustan, a world where a crossing guard run over by a carjacker is not regarded as the victim, but rather the carjacker—an agencyless zombie driven to this specific act by long dead white men—is the victim.

Your moral code does not apply.

# 'The Translator'

## An Hour with the Enemy of Humanity—of My Own Blood

© 2016 James LaFond

A few years back I was at a cousin's wedding, speaking to a second cousin, an attractive young woman who had a master's degree in Spanish. This was in 2011, when I was writing a novel about a time traveler to16th century Florida. I was thrilled to speak with her, as I only knew from my Mexican fighter and Puerto Rican coach, that people from different Central American nations had different dialects of Spanish that were mutually intelligible, but featured some different words and usages. When with these men the conversation was always weighted toward combat and I had gleaned nothing of these things, least of all the difference between Castilian, the lingua franca of most of the conquistadors and Spanish as spoken today.

For instance, if I had a modern Puerto Rican time traveler speaking to Soto, what stumbling blocks might there be in the way of Amerindian loan words and modern developments that might make understanding less than smooth, or at least humorous?

My cousin went on to explain that there were no Spanish dialects, that there was but one way of speaking Spanish and that all Latinos were as one and of one mind. [I mused silently that this would obviously explain the lack of civil wars and insurgencies in South and Central America.]

I countered that people from Baltimore, London, New York, Pittsburg, Antigua, Trinidad and Australia, which I had known, all spoke different regional dialects, and that surely, there is a word that modern Mexicans say that Christopher Columbus would not have recognized?

No, all Latinos and Latinas speak thee exact universal dialect of Spanish, and that furthermore they are all globalists, honest and morally superior to hate-filled white Americans.

I pointed out that ancient Greek was spoken in Ionian, Attic, Dorian, Koine [a military/trade dialect], and two other dialects I cannot recall.

She assured me that such differences in language only persist with American English, because America is the land of bigotry, separatism and racism enforced by white prejudice, and that other languages are all spoken in unified globalist harmony.

What? I thought, as she dragged me down the rabbit hole of her agenda.

It turned out, that she had gone to work for an organization devoted to providing health care, drivers licenses, housing and citizenship to illegal aliens and had fallen in love and become engaged to a man from Honduras, I think—hopefully he's not Salvadoran!

I have since met a person who speaks and teaches Spanish, who assured me that this woman either lied about her degree or about her experience, as the language has certain regional and national nuances that makes studying with certain "native speakers" both fascinating and challenging. Yes, when she took over ordering at the authentic Mexican restaurant, she and the owner could make themselves understood, but, it seemed—by their facial expressions and body language—like I was listening to a New Englander speak with a West Virginian. It looked to me like they both enjoyed the interaction, partially because they were both experiencing something like a differentiated kinship, an expansion of their individual lingual elasticity. In them, I saw such a world which has always existed, in various tones of joy and sorrow. In my cousin, I saw the evil monotone chrome that threatens to coat the human mind—like a thugess with blindingly gray spray paint tagging the Mono Lisa as she calls Leonardo a sexist.

Readers: if you are a Spanish speaker, I was wondering, can you provide an example of a word used in one nation or dialect that is not understood by this proposed universal, Leftist, Hispanic mind?

## 'Crabs Pull Each Other Down the Pot'

**Rappers and Celebrity Criminals Preach Urban Flight from Baltimore**

© 2016 James LaFond

Of the half dozen local ghetto celebrity thugs who spoke at four Baltimore city schools last year in the wake of the publicized riots and the secretive race Purge, half have been shot or jailed and the other half are leaving Harm City ASAP!

Recently, Tyriece Watson, who went by a name more inane than this ghetto tag, was gunned down. At his West Baltimore vigil, police showed up to demonstrate solidarity and were attacked [mildly] by his infantile death cult.

Now, Justin Fenton [a real Baltimore reporter] has [in the 6/29/16 issue of The Baltimore Sun] scored an interview with some Dindu named Braxton, who has been shot in the head twice since speaking out against gang violence, and is preaching hip hop flight into the suburbs, which should really alarm you white rabbits in the hills above Dindustan, which shall soon be annexed by these hip hop heroes, who, despite Hitler's claim that they are just animals that cannot be outrun by a man, do not seem capable of outrunning their toxic culture any more than the fleeing white rabbits they pursue.

Three Notes:

1. The crabs he is speaking of are no longer affordable to working class and middle class people, only to the elite and the criminals, ranging up to $120 a dozen.

2. The Freddie Gray case is leaking at the burst seams.

3. Dindu mammas—kind of like their brutal feminist war priests—are in the streets calling for the conviction of a white cop for the death of Martyr Gray.

# 'The Knockers'
## Tia's Ghetto Heroes

© 2016 James LaFond

"Back in the mid-nineties, when I was living with my mom and stepfather, we moved from East Baltimore around Hopkins—which was way too violent to live in—over to Harford and Twenty-fifth. But it was bad over there too, even though you could see the Courthouse. Those Cherry Hill boys would be up in their beefing—fussing with the local thugs. My step brother was killed by drug dealers. That set my stepfather off. We called him Dad. He really tried, really cared. He would say hello to the thugs and drug dealers on his way down to the store, but when he saw them dealing he would get on the phone and implicate us. We were so afraid we would get shot or burned up over this—and did eventually move out into the county.

"One time he was out on the porch with the cordless phone yelling to the 911 operator so the drug dealers could hear, giving their descriptions. Oh my God, we were terrified!"

[This was between 94-98, when a house full of women at Erdman and Edison were executed by the Hugo Boyz—a crew that operated out of this neighborhood just below Harford and Hugo, where the corner house still looks like a gated asylum—and during which time I collected most of the stories that appear in When You're Food. ]

"My heroes were The Knockers. The Knockers is what we called them, because they came in plain clothes and knocked them hoodlums in the head. They were black narcotics officers. They got this one boy that was dealing drugs in front of our house. When he swallowed his dope, they used a pen and put it down his throat to make him gag. Then, when he threw it up, they walked around holding his product up, telling everyone around that he was charging double what the same thing sold for in West Baltimore, and that it was poor quality and he was just a chump, had been run out of the Westside for selling low-quality stuff.

"I stayed in sports and music in school to stay out of trouble. Then the gangs took over the schools so we had to move to the county, where they are taking over the schools now. The entire time on Harford and twenty-fifth, the only time I felt safe outside on the porch was when The Knockers, came, whooping ass, knocking heads and taking thugs away. Now, I'm working three jobs and living with my grandmother, ten darn miles out of the city, where she has lived her entire eighty years—and here they come, like roaches on the bus, the thugs, with their guns and bullshit to drive us out again."

[As I checked these notes from my conversation with Tia on the way back into town, the Valentino Crew was not out in force at Northern and Harford. They were all scattered, glaring at the single black cop that stood there with his arms crossed, scaring off their customers. I saw two deals being made back in the neighborhood, but the civilians could at least use the buses for so long as he stuck around.]

# 'In Armed America'
## The Three Prongs of AnarchoTyranny in Your Local Newspaper

© 2016 James LaFond

I spent the past two days out of town with family. Knowing that I will be deluged via TV and newspaper with mainstream mind-feed for the moral chattel of The Lie, I brought two books on dreams and shamanism, which I read, giving me an antidote and a barometer for the insanity that my blood does not know that they are immersed in.

My mother has saved me a copy of the Baltimore Sun's editorial page from Thursday, June 23. After I looked at it she was taking it into work to show her coworkers, as a former colleague of hers had made good and was featured in her own editorial, a picture of her [a middle-aged, white professor of business]

98

flashing a gang sign next to a thug rapper. My mother merely thought this was "cute."

I said, "Mom, do you think she realizes that this guy has robbed white people, beat up homeless black men and probably participated in the gang-rape of a twelve-year-old black girl, in order to qualify for his social status?"

Mom winced as she flipped the blueberry pancakes, "Probably not—she's highly educated, though."

I read the article about investing in inner city rap music and that hip hop [which this woman is studying as practitioner of this rarified art] is an "overlooked" cultural resource.

I then looked to the other articles. One was by a young activist, who is trying to eliminate prison terms and jail time for criminals with children. [Which would equate to a reproductive pardon for every Dindu over 13] It is based on her chasing the police car within which her father rode away to his 11-year term.

The third piece was an anti-gun article, touting the disarmament of all law abiding citizens as the only way to stop the violence being committed by criminals. This man was a philosophy professor at a Baltimore Art College.

I explained to my mother what this meant, how important this single page was to anyone interested in the dissolution of morality and community in the Western World.

The philosopher preaches individual and community disarmament.

The economist preaches criminal empowerment.

The activist preaches criminal absolution.

The aggregate of their initiatives, should they gain currency, would be a free range criminal habitat, within which the disarmed citizen will be helpless and utterly dependent on government protection, seeking cover under the ever more distant umbrella of State security, which recedes by fits and starts from local, to state, to federal, to global, even as The State cultivates and imports criminal threats, which the philosopher excuses, the economist encourages and the activist forgives.

# Tampons or Maxi-Pads?
### 'The Recent Riot or Incident out in Sacramento, California': A Man Question from Chris

© 2016 James LaFond

James

I like your site and writing. Thanks and please keep going.

I was wondering if you could share any thoughts on the recent riot or incident out in Sacramento, California.

For instance, look at the still photo of the video at this link:

http://www.reuters.com/video/2016/06/26/sacramento-stabbing-victim-says-nazis-re?videoId=369079074&newsChannel=topNews

Is that guy in the tan pants wearing everything I suspect he might be wearing? Why? What is that belt thing? What could be in its pockets? What's could be in his right thigh pants pocket—looks boxy? Is he wearing some sort of fighting glove?

As for the politics, I wonder if both "sides" are loaded with government agent provocateurs.

Although obviously there is some legal aspect to all this.

But I'm wondering what thoughts you could share.

Thanks

-Chris

Thank you, Chris.

I think the Jews have a saying of encouragement for both combatant parties when two of their enemies go at it, which would apply here. The guy who was the backbone of the Right Wing resistance here, tried stirring up shit in my town and is associated with groups that evolved from the earlier skinhead movement that put me in its cross hairs and nearly slew my innocent cousin. On the other hand, the

Leftists here were recently agitating Dindu hordes in Baltimore to attack white people, including me. So I hope both sides inflict maximum casualties, and although I am retired from boxing and stick fighting, would be willing to fight to the death [totally serious here] with bowie knives with any member of either party, should they care to lodge a challenge. That would be a video that would get me a lot of posthumous book sales!

Now let me examine the still link:

http://www.reuters.com/video/2016/06/26/sacramento-stabbing-victim-says-nazis-re?videoId=369079074&newsChannel=topNews

Okay. I don't know anything about this at the point I am writing. It seems that the red beret faggot, with his weight on his rear leg, has advanced in a defensive posture, trying to illicit an attack. Okay I could take out three of him with my case cutter. Seriously—he's a non-combatant in my book. Whatever he has in his back pocket—tampons or maxipads, I can't tell—is not for combat. The "belt thing" is a back brace, like I wear at work and if this ass would synch up the Velcro closure in front would be decent armor against small blade slashes. If fastened around the waist it can protect against a slash or rip cut, but not a good stab. He looks to be wearing plain old dress gloves, although it could be something better, like sap gloves, in either case making the stick a liability.

The grungy, bald dudes are also in a defensive posture with hands obviously pocketing knives. The big guy is either wearing fingerless gloves, okay in a fight and don't really hinder weapon handling. They seem to be grinning to themselves, "Come here Che, so I can shank you off camera." The stabber looks to be the smaller guy on their right. I would guess the bigger dude to his left is the door jammer. I would type both of them for carrying folding tactical knives, with the small guy more likely to put it up your ass.

The Asian chick as spokesperson is a good idea from the Lefties. If more right wing guys could lay in good dick we'd have less of these unfulfilled cunts to babble at us. Seriously, convert a couple of Caucasian porn stars to the cause and send them into these colleges and these bitches will revert to the slutdom they were designed for.

With the decent quality looking muscle of the skin heads I think the knives are a mistake. A choice of sticks of such length marks incapable combatants. A few wrestler-boxer types could clean out a platoon of these beret-wearing nimrods. Remember, this time last year teenage kids with rocks defeated police armed in the same fashion. Empty hand is really more effective than stick unless you are an actual stick fighter and there are less than a hundred of us in the U.S.

When reading these situations look for who has their shoulders raised and who has relaxed shoulders. By that measure the two skinheads can hit and the faggot with the stick probably has a hard time jerking off with his left hand.

I will check some other sources, Chris—my emails seem full of this stuff.

Thanks for the support.

Below is a link that Mescaline Franklin sent me. Apparently Vox is covering this.

The good video has been taken down.

Look, seriously, if you had five cohesive men: two big, one smart and two dangerous, you could route armies of these kind of people without weapons from a wedge formation. I personally know five guys who knockout everybody they hit every time unless the guy they hit is a freak. All you need is two of them, two big flankers and a coordinator—that is until the opposition gets some experience. Right now it seems that the Left is limited to recruiting live action role playing nerds.

https://voxday.blogspot.com/2016/06/be-prepared-this-summer.html

# Dinduology #1

## Announcing A Free, Unaccredited Course on the Predatory Habits of the World's Most Domesticated Hunter

© 2016 James LaFond

Forget the nature shows you saw when you were a kid. There is no hierarchy of competing predators, like hyenas running off vultures and lions whacking hyenas. One must instead imagine a predation scenario in which the lions pull security for the hyenas as the vultures harass you!

Absolutely do not bother with reruns of Deadliest Warrior, for Dindus are not warriors, do not fight, but hunt. However, Dindus cannot hunt in an intact ecosystem. They are too fragile and must hunt in the hen house. No beast of prey is more domesticated, more utterly dependent on the help of other predators then the Dindu.

Forget Habitat Hoodrat! Yes, Dindus are too soft for Habitat Hoodrat and are fleeing to Dindustan, where they will enjoy police protection, garden apartments with actual grass and mudsharks who cannot get enough Dindu D...!

As I travel back and forth from Habitat Hoodrat to suburban Dindustan, aggression patterns are beginning to differentiate.

Before we continue, here is the pop quiz of the day: where is the most dangerous place to be, during the day, if you are a law abiding pedestrian in Dindustan?

The answer is the subject of our next post. Feel free to post your answer before 7/1/16 to test your powers of Dinduology!

# Dinduology #2
## Where is the Most Dangerous Place for a Law-Abiding Civilian in Dindustan?

© 2016 James LaFond

Let's take the recently overrun Parkville Precinct of Baltimore County. One would think that the safest place to be in a beleaguered municipal subdivision would be at the "fort" the strongpoint from which the "Cavalry" in blue sally forth "to protect and serve."

This would be the case, if the 8th Precinct at Old Harford Road and Putty Hill were an infantry station, like a 19th century police barracks for foot patrolmen. But modern policing is based around the automobile, with officers as dispersed as possible. In the case of the vast Parkville Precinct, the largest zip code in the Greater Baltimore area, nearly half the size of the entire city, with officers busy fighting to keep city criminals south of the City Line, the "cavalry" from "the fort" are all dispersed to the frontier. What is more is that Baltimore Area police precincts know that their headquarters are gang and terrorist targets and are therefore not places you simply waltz into.

The cohesive aspect of modern policing is remote communication, beginning with the victim or witness phoning in for help. This makes the police dispatch hub a manpower dead zone, except for three one hour blocks around shift change, with officers on the patrol on the regional perimeter and the dispatch of these officers to trouble spots based on phone calls, not a knock on the door by a witness or victim of a crime conducted on the precinct doorstep. Dindus, of course, understand this better than their victims, and always take a prey's cell phone.

Over the past two weeks seven mobs of Dindus have attacked, beaten, threatened and/or robbed civilians within sight [or a 1 minute walk] of the 8th Precinct!

The pigs penned there have admitted to three of these attacks and have either not reported or otherwise obscured the location of the other attacks. Such attacks have also been occurring near the Essex and White Marsh precincts, with those in Essex going back six years. The zone immediately around the Essex precinct is the most lightly patrolled section of the area of responsibility, with the major bus transfer hub a quarter mile away so crime ridden that the bus shelters are rarely used and pedestrians are mob attacked weekly and homeowners have suffered repeated home invasions–reclassified as burglaries or robberies.

This is similar to muggers and rapists staking out municipal courthouses, as they know that distracted women will be forever spewing forth from the facility after filing for child support, divorce, peace orders and marriage licenses, as well as jurors, who, in the city, are set out helpless on the street as the gangbangers associated with the gangbanger on trial wait to have a word with them—or worse.

Cops are not conditioned to look for, or even recognize, crime at their work hub, with a cop headed to the 7-11 for a soda before he begins patrolling numbering among the least aware of his kind. Court is even more distracting for cops. Dindus know that civilians do not understand such things, and, like any self-serving predator, choose a time and place to strike which is least expected by their next meal.

So, when your suburban refuge is annexed to Dindustan, do not walk past the local police precinct expecting its shadow to cast a protective spell over you.

Oh, and do not forget, if you get attacked by a pack of Dindus in front of the police station [like Andy Yo-Clocker, who was threatened by the police for defending himself earlier this year], and you manage to successfully defend yourself, if any cop coming or going notices, he will probably see you engaged in the most criminal act that a citizen of Dindustan can commit—self defense against the oppressed. Victims of your pale privilege!

Cracker, don't you know that you're just food?

## Dinduology #3
### On the Dinduball Court

© 2016 James LaFond

Nottingham is the very picture of soulless, postmodern America:

prefabricated town homes, McMansions, strip malls with 100% national chains operating in bustling profusion, paved sidewalks with wheelchair ramps along every street, regular bus service provided by the #58, and #35, with a commuter bus shuttle stop from Harford County, five minute interstate access to I-95 and the second largest movie theater in Maryland, at The Avenue,

But over the past year, violent crime and burglary rates have surged with a huge influx of Baltimore City residents. Some of these new arrivals are fatherless welfare families with section 8 vouchers. But most of

113

the new arrivals are fleeing the ghettos of Baltimore City via the #35 bus line, which serves Franklin Square hospital and the adjacent Community College. The typical family unit has two to three earners, one a mother and the other two either adult children or a boyfriend of the mother or adult daughter.

Last year Mantrell moved out to Nottingham with his mother, who works at Franklin Square Hospital down the street. At 19 he is enrolled in Baltimore County Community College and works at one of the shops at The Avenue at White Marsh, an easy walk or five minute drive from his mother's large town home. Being out in the county is so much better than being in the city. He can actually—well could—walk around without getting jacked like he always did around Perkins Homes when his mother worked at Hopkins. However, Mantrell has a car. Things are—sorry, were—were going good.

Mantrell figured he'd take advantage of the mild, mid-June, weekday afternoon and stop by the community basketball court to shoot some hoops before heading into work. In Baltimore City boxing gyms have always been safer places for young men than basketball courts, but this is the suburbs!

There were some dudes playing on the court and as he was walking in, three younger dudes—still in high school—stepped up to him and demanded everything he had. One of them was a big, mean dude, so he handed over his cash out of his wallet –this was cool, that they didn't demand his license and cards—and his keys and phone. He thought they were going to take his phone and his car, but they smashed the phone and keys and left them with him. The other dudes on the court just went about their business so he walked home, got his spare keys, had his mom bring him up to get his car, then he called the cops and filed a report when they came out to speak with him. The episode made him late for work.

**Dindu Behaviors**

1. Dindus know that few bystanders will aid the victim or speak to the cops.

2. Basketball courts are the best place to jack someone, because the hip hop code of silence reigns amongst basketball players. Never move into an area that has a functional basketball court. If a basketball court is installed in your community, remove the hoops and nets. Most players will go elsewhere.

3. When Dindus move into a new hunting zone they seek out prey that resembles them, so that they might wet their fangs on easy kills as their eventual victims look the other way. Also, attacking non criminals who have been indoctrinated into the urban code of silence, is an ideal risk limiting strategy.

4. Phones and keys will be taken by intelligent Dindu foot patrols [the keys especially if you are black, as you might have a gun in your car] to discourage you from pursuing or shooting them and preventing a timely call to police or friends.

5. Black men, keep in mind that Dindus put more thought into attacking you than they do into attacking whites, who are assumed to be easy prey. You should use this in your avoidance strategy, beginning with leaving the Dinduball courts alone. Also, keep in mind that most cops will run a check on you for warrants before they even take down your description of the criminals.

# Dinduology #4
## Seamus and the Rookie Reparations Recovery Agents

© 2016 James LaFond

In June Seamus was walking away from Golden Ring mall, heading over to Route 40, when a juvenile Dindu approached him on the sidewalk and lifted his T-shirt, showing an automatic handgun in the waistband of his lime green shorts.

At this time Seamus noticed that a Dindu adult in a car was shadowing him at a walking pace. The youth with the un-deployed firearm said, "Give it up, yo," as he puffed out his scrawny chest.

Seamus responded by stepping off into the street, walking down the center line and dialing 911 on his cell, while asking the twerp on the sidewalk, "What caliber is that?"

To that, as Seamus executed the best strategy for avoiding a gunman in Dinduurbia, there was no answer other than the squealing of the car tires and the, "Oh shit, yo!" of the fleeing, pint-sized gunman, who was not picked up by his accomplice as he fled the other way.

So, my Dindu bruthas, when you tool up and pack-out to go collect reparations, please preserve our dignity by not fleeing and screaming like a bitch, from an un-armed cracker at that!

# 'Is Baltimore Safe for Street Musicians?'

## Rachel Wants to Know If She Will Ever See Such a Hipsteriffic Sight in Harm City

© 2016 James LaFond

Street musicians are rare in Harm City, Rachel, but they exist. Now street rappers, you can find doing their headset mixes at every bus stop. As far as singing and playing instruments, there are two that I know of.

There is Sol, who hauls his plastic milk crate with money bucket and vodka bottle around in his left hand and carries his acoustic guitar in his right. His blues is good and his classic rock better. He plays outside of liquor stores—or did, until he beat up Aldo's roommate and skipped town. He could take care of himself and I'd pity any hoodrat that tried to dip a hand in his money can, wherever it sits at present.

Recently, on Mothers say, I was down Fells Point when a suave, black, heavy metal guitarist who played a lot of Clapton and some Led Zeppelin on an electric guitar for which he had his own power source, set up on the brick median right across from the merchant's square. He targeted his music to his audience, was pleasant, took requests, had an impressive Mohawk fade, did not sing at all, favoring rhythm over lead and would have been robbed, rolled, stomped and left lay for an ambulance in most neighborhoods where he looks like he would belong.

So yes, Rachel, street musicians can survive in Harm City. They just have to find out where You and Yours wine and dine, so that They might escape the cruel attention of Theirs.

# The Blessing of WellRead Ed
**Our Correspondent from North Dindustan**
**Muses on Behalf of Tenacious Curmudgeons**

© 2016 WelRead Ed & James LaFond

Just a few thoughts while I contemplate the universe:

I'm sure you must tire of people asking, "Why do you do it? Why do you live in Baltimore?" But I get it. Living as a Lion in the jungle is gratifying. Hyenas give even old Lions a wide berth; they know that being maimed or killed because you and your posse wanted to take down an Alpha Predator is not a positive outcome. And BEING that Alpha Predator is a pleasant sensation, indeed.

Being a tool-using Primate just prolongs your Era of Lethality. Most people, even the dimmest of the Dindus, are not prepared to deal with someone that is willing and able to employ utter, remorseless, ruthlessness. Knockout Game Players cannot fathom that someone would be willing to gouge out their eye, or bite their ear off. The idea that an intended victim, especially palefaces, would be willing to drive several inches of heat-treated steel between their ribs is as foreign a concept to them as The Pythagorean Theorem.

If you study the patterns of predators, 2-legged and 4-legged have remarkably similar tactics; separate the prey from the group, cut off escape routes, attack from multiple angles simultaneously, when the prey falls, pile on and finish it. However, if the prey mounts an effective resistance, either by being faster than the pack or by making it obvious that further pursuit will be costly in energy and resources, they quickly lose interest.

Regrettably, most paleface males have become grass eaters; as defenseless against predators as cattle on The Savanna, because they have been conditioned by soft males, emasculated schools, and pop culture that stomping the ankle of an attacker that you have knocked to the ground is wrong. To even suggest a thing causes them to recoil in horror.

And you revel in that 'edge' you have over people living in more docile environs. (here, is where I venture into psycho-philosophy, completely without qualification or education in either) You, as someone who has no such compunctions, walk as a Lion among Jackals. You take no unnecessary risks, but you are aware that, as age and decrepitude take their toll, someday you might succumb to the pack, you still live in the jungle because you know that your life will not be taken cheaply, and that whatever God(s) you subscribe to will be watching whether you go out as a man or not. To die while leaving your enemies with scars, limps, the corpses of their allies, and the nagging fear that there might be more like you is, in my humble opinion, a good death.

Blessings,

WellRead Ed

Here's to a good death!


Thank you, Ed.

I must admit that part of the appeal of being a relative "lion" in such a debased culture is that I can. Three hundred years ago, I'm just another dog in the pack, like the slave that started my family's American journey. But with Dindus instead of Iroquois to battle, I can play the lion as a mangy mutt—even getting on in years. If there is a god of irony in that pantheon I'm trying to locate, maybe he'll approve. But if Drake is looking down he'd spit at me and ask Saint Peter for a day pass so he could cut me down in a duel.

Bro, I'll take it.

The other thing that is oh so much fun, is dealing with suburbanites. Most cops are suburbanites, by the way. The one cop I train asked me last week, "Seriously, Mister LaFond—respectfully—when you bring it in sparring, I can tell you like the dirty stuff. So, let's say you step outside tonight, and some dude just brings it. No posing, no bullshit—in your work boots, needing to get things done. What is your go to move?"

I showed him:

"A southpaw jab, open hand to the skull if his head is ducked, or if he is upright, a spear to the eyes. I practice it about forty times a day behind a weak pivot. The entire response is based on diverting his attention to his eyes so I can shoulder check him with my palm and sweep his ankle with the boot."

He countered, "What about your finish, how do you envision finishing a guy headed to the floor?"

"I envision it every day and every night and practice it when I shadow box alone. As soon as my man begins heading to the floor I need to now he's not getting back up, because there will be others. When he goes timber I estimate where his hips are going to hit and then crouch leap as high as I can, landing with a double heel thrust on his pelvis or abdomen. I want to error on the abdomen if off target and not turn my ankle on a thigh. If the knives are out or it's in my home I target the head for the leaping stomp."

He looked at me with scrunched eyebrows, "Jesus, brother, how about when I'm not on duty! I don't even want to see what's left."

So, my WellRead friend, just what I have to visualize and practice to prevail in the poor odds encounters that are most likely [if I fail in my avoidance efforts], strikes a creepy note even to the ears of experienced cops and if I didn't like creeping people out I wouldn't write horror.

# 'Unshackled Youth'
## Maryland Court of Appeals Upholds Motion to Free the Oppressed from Their Unjust Chains

© 2016 James LaFond

"Just in at the Dinustan News Desk, innocent, unarmed, Dindu youth to be free, free at last!

"Jungle Jim here, to assure you guilt ridden residents of Whitebreadistan, that your client thugs in Dindustan will now be unshackled when they appear before the judge. The question is, what does this signify? Let me turn the keyboard over to renowned Dinduologist, Webone Shoop.

"Well Webone, what's up with the shackles coming off?"

"Yeah, this is the kind of thing you white folks wouldn't know anything about. It's pretty simple, really, JayJay, that is if you can set your prejudice aside for just a moment and consider the complexity of Dindu diction. Now, would you expect some Italian chef to go on and on about expeller pressed olive oil without using his hands? No, you would not, because his ass is almost entirely white—so he gets a pass. Yet, with just a little bit of black in him, you understand that that Italian scallion needs some hands in the mix to be understood at the nuanced level.

"So, if my man, Crinkle be pleading his case in front of Judge Jewy, we are talking about more nuances than any Tuscan sauté. I mean how's an undergraduate of shit-ass public schools gonna sell, "Serious yo Hona, I jus' seen Scotta go down like dat—I dindu nuffin!"

"Thank you, Webone Shoop, for that insightful tutorial!"

R.I.P. Scoota, here's a forty to you, son.

# This Week in Dindustan
### Jungle Jim Reviews Dindu News from Harm City and Harm County

© 2016 James LaFond

On all fronts, those who dindu nuffin have made strides—or have had them made for them as they slept off that nasty Steel Reserve hangover—on this glorious early summer week:

-Baltimore County Police are now wearing cameras, so, so...well, hopefully that will work to Dindu advantage, just saying that we should try and be optimistic while remaining careful.

-The Baltimore City Police Department will spend $370,000 on gunfire censors, so that they will know where the caps are being busted and make sure they go the other goddamned way.

-In June 2016, the most dangerous place to take an afternoon stroll in Baltimore County was in front of the 8th District Precinct at Putty Hill and Old Harford Road in Parkville.

-The Baltimore City Police Department is now embracing "the sanctity of life" as a policing philosophy. There is no news as to whether the rumor is true that Jain religious advisors will be brought in from Southern India for advice on wearing insect protection masks. Come on, Webone, it is to protect the insects—they got life in them too!

-Baltimore City rappers are advising that any Dindu who can afford it flee Baltimore City, as the Dundids [figure it out] seem to be ratcheting up their hip hop manhunt.

-Baltimore County has got this fit, baby doll cop named Miesha, with a badass, apple-bobbing ponytail, so hopefully her cute ass will be pulling your dumb ass over this July 4th holiday weekend instead of Officer Joebob.

-The Chief of Baltimore police has asked that you deal your drugs in front of the blue light camera stands, not behind them, or in the blind spots caused by the school walls. So please, do your part.

-The Maryland Court of Appeals has outlawed the shackling of gangbanging young hoppers.

-Home invasions and robberies are increasingly being reported as burglaries in Baltimore County. So if you're working in the stickup trade, try job rotation and go in for some home invasions, which should be aided by...

-A bunch of dumb, rich, crackers and a few praying fools are pushing for new gun restrictions in Maryland, which will hopefully help us increase our H.I. numbers. [No, Webone, I'm not one of you, but my readership is built on the dumb shit you do, so I am concerned!] Let's just hope that they don't find out that the guns are not sentient, ambulatory assassins, but merely weapons.

# Through a Glass Snarkly
### Dependence Day Eve in Dindustan

© 2016 James LaFond

On July 1 EBT cash came out; $250 per neglected child.

Only July 5, those whose last names begin with A, B and C will get the "food side" of their card loaded.

But for now, on the eve of this nation's anniversary, when I was hoping to have finished out the day with a nap, the damp, cool, summer night air is crackling with dundididmaself fireworks.

The roommate's girl is yelling at him for being a dude—which I had thought was the entire point of his birth.

I'm too tired to write reviews or impressions of any of the 14 chapters and stories stacked up on the air filter.

I feel incomplete, having wanted to do a number of things today.

Oliver did his sprints in between jobs today, so I didn't get to demonstrate silverback knuckle running to the young bull.

I have had a copy of one book each for Hawk and Quinn, two older fellows I see at the mixed race sports bar. I considered dropping the books off at the bar and stapled them in envelopes this afternoon. But, I had boxing articles to write and I was so tired that if I had one beer it would have ruined me and if they were there when I stopped in I wouldn't want to be rude and just walk off. It's been since February I think, since I've seen them.

I wanted to stop down this evening after I was too tired to write anything decent, but I don't feel like rolling the dice and coming up snake eyes, which is about the odds that I'd have any problem with hoodlums tonight. Some other time. I'll take my walk at 4 a.m.

This morning I was headed to breakfast after work in the passenger seat of Capri's new pink minibus with the gray primer flowers, when she actually stopped for the yellow light instead of disparaging rival motorists as she ripped through. This gave me time to regard the yellow house—a house I did not realize until this morning was yellow, even though I have seen it hundreds of times. When I have time to stop and consider a frame house, of the kind that one finds on country roads in Maryland and Pennsylvania, with a yawing porch reminding me of a mouth and nose and two upstairs windows seeming like eyes under the pointy crown, I wonder about the people stuck inside, which is how I have always thought of people, stuck inside, like me sitting between book stacks and drinking cheap beer while...

*Some asshole across the street just cut loose with a 3.57 magnum, which made my heart sink...*

Well, I just looked at that house knowing that it had been there long before that 75 by 75 yard patch off asphalt where four streets [one of them schizophrenic and two others dying of loneliness] and three parking lots merge into one forever empty space...

*And the dickhead down the street is popping off his .22 auto as if size really doesn't matter...*

So, as Capri pulled through the intersecting moonscape without a tree or a bush obscuring the house from this view of road tar, I mused, "Imagine, waking up every morning for years, for decades and looking out that front door—at this."

Capri laughed out loud, uncontrollably and almost ran over some tiny Dindu, who she cursed, "Oh get out of my way—you don't even speak a real language!" and then smiled rosily at me and quipped, "You just can't help yourself, can you?"

I proved her right, after a fashion, "Never fear, Baby—every cloud has a gray taint and I'm here to remind you."

So, please, to the readers that somehow found themselves here, at the end of the internet, to sort through the downloading of a damaged brain, yes, its terminal, and I can't help it, but wouldn't if I could.

# The Presidential Infestation
## A Man Question from Mouse on the Next American President

© 2016 James LaFond

"James, Stefan Molyneux is stumping for Trump. Are you Libertarian? Are you going to vote for Trump or Thor or what?"

-Mouse

I am a slave of the world's greatest plantation yet. Others might pretend that when the overseer, who represents the unseen slave master, tells me that I can have a fractional voice in the running of the plantation, that I am being given a choice. I prefer a more proactive relationship to fiction. As a prisoner of the United States, who is currently in violation of letting his slave pass expire, I can be arrested at any time for walking down the street with an expired Maryland State I.D. I count myself as a marooned observer in an insane world. It makes my friends feel better to vote, so I encourage them to do so.

The U.S. is clearly a debt-driven oligarchy. It, like every nation, always elevates the leader it deserves. My opinion, is that since the primary characteristic of the current United States of America, when compared to previous manifestations of this polity, is emasculation, then it should be ruled by a queen. I further contend that any queen worth the name is evil, must be evil if she is truly to serve the cause of keeping humans imprisoned on this single planet.

I believe that America is, psychologically and morally, a polity weakened to the point of anemia and that it deserves a queen, a queen most terrible, an autarch with the amoral ferocity to finally tear aside the curtain of nationhood and lay bare the machinery of perpetual enthrallment. I would count myself lucky, if in my lifetime, I was able to look up and see what our ancestors certainly saw with much more clarity than we, from beneath this heavily curtained stage: naked power, so beautifully corrupt as to exert an amoral gravity of such density that truth will warp like light bent around a light-extinguishing immensity.

It would be a wonder to behold Queen Cunt's diabolic ascent to her gilded perch and we would be blessed to witness Her wrathful rule.

## 'Home of the Brave'
### Two Minutes at Harford Road and Evergreen on the Fourth of July

© 2016 James LaFond

At 10:24 I headed down to the ghetto mart for avocados. Few vehicles were using Harford Road and none were active on the side streets. This is Sunday with a hangover. The two elderly, handicapped regulars—two black folks who worked into their seventies and are now retired in their eighties—await the #19 to downtown under the shade of the old tree sprouting from the sidewalk before the Maryland State Health Department building. As I stepped on the bricks being heaved up slowly by the determined tree, he smiled and waved and I nodded.

The intersection of Evergreen and Harford looms ahead—the center of Hamilton proper, although Hamilton Avenue is two blocks away—as I walk next to and past the concrete Hamilton Bank and come out next to the ATM, where I have been threatened and challenged by Dindus five times in the past three years. With no pedestrians out, I decide to take in the sights.

The Pakistani gas station, where drugs are openly dealt and men use the lot by the air pump as a private open air garage to detail their cars, is across Harford to my left. On that side of Harford Evergreen is one lane, spilling into the main drag between the air pump and the optimistically painted Hamilton School for the Performing Arts, where numerous crews of thugs have used the sidewalk and parking spot for a staging area from which to launch attacks on those palefaces using this ATM machine, behind me, next to a flight of stairs where patrolling cops have long permitted groups of young thugs to congregate close enough to count a customer's money.

The entire area is clean, free of trash, as the leader of the Hamilton Business Association pays a janitor to clean the four block expanse. Towering overhead, across this two-lane stretch of Evergreen [a side street comprised of numerous dead ends that winds and wanders like a broken stick across Northeast

Baltimore] is the Hamilton Presbyterian Church, whose pastor is handy with the thematic holiday saying placed on the low, five-line marquee before the old stone steps.

I walk over to read this admonishment and am intrigued:

"This nation shall remain the land of the free only so long as it is the home of the brave."

I like it, feeling almost American as the anachronistic truism soaks into my soul.

*Excuse me, my roommate's woman is throwing stuff and screaming. I let her put Gibbon's Decline and Fall of the Roman Empire in her glass china cabinet, so must go downstairs and make sure the old sage's bound words are not being weaponized...*

As I mused over this local religious leader's choice of words, from up the rising elevation of Evergreen, down out of the crackhouse-infested west, shuffled what looked like Fat Albert in a militant black power hooded sweat shirt. He was mumbling his raps loud enough to himself to be nearly audible to me from 60 yards in the absence of traffic.

I turned and regarded the young person as I began to walk down the flanking church stairs into the grassy churchyard, between this dignified looking edifice, the rectory and the hall, where services are actually held. As soon as I directed my steps down the stairs the voice of the giant toddler—perhaps 6 feet three inches and 360 pounds, and looking in the face to be about 15—amplified his volume to a shrieking scream, one hand holding something in his sweat shirt pocket and the other flashing gang signs.

The sweatshirt was a legitimate garment for this cool, overcast day, threatening storm. But, as I walked down the seven stairs, the only storm within earshot was:

"Yo muthafuca, where da bitch be yo steppin'! Dis is da real nigga, hea, da real nigga, yo hea, da muvafucin cracka-crushin' nigga—ya hea! I will fuck you up Old School; da nine be muvafucin mine, bitch!..."

More words came at less volume as I turned the stone corner of the building that had once echoed better songs and smiled, because my "Saint Patrick Shrub" I call it was occupied. This is a large, box-cut, evergreen shrub against the back church wall, where I have sighted numerous juvenile rabbits over the years and where sparrows congregate and raise their young. They chirp from within, making it like a giant muffled music box. I looked for "my buddy" but did not find him. For the past three weeks a juvenile sparrow which seems disinclined to fly, perched at the fist-sized opening boldly, regarding me as I walked back and forth in the morning, even turning its head to follow my progress as I passed. Hopefully he's flying today.

From there the only sounds I heard were my sneakers on the sandy concrete, the blubbery toad of a rapper lost behind me.

# Losing Face in Dinduspace
## A Note On Censorship from our FaceBook Moderator

© 2016 James LaFond

James,

I think facebook is censoring us now. I have tried posting articles to the page and they are not posting with any heading or information whatsoever. Only the link of the website will pop up. I tried posting your articles on my own page and it worked just fine. However, this isn't the first time your material has been censored on facebook. I recall trying to post an article that mentioned Black Lives Matter and the same thing happened. This could be a hassle to resolve. Just letting you know.

-Bart

https://www.facebook.com/tabooyou

Bart, I really appreciate what you have been doing with the FaceBook site, as I had no stomach for it. Even this news is valuable and of interest. Don't get yourself in any trouble on my account, but please continue the probe into this. It would be an honor to be banished from social media, so please continue. More importantly, keep us up to date on your warrior journey: fights and training, that matters more to us than all of the bleeding hearts in Dindustan.

James

# A Forty for Lor Scoota
**Death in Dindustan**

© 2016 James LaFond

Last week Harm City was rocked with the tragic death of aspiring rapper, Tyriece Watson, otherwise known as "Lor Scoota." The killing sparked a call by fellow rappers to their friends and neighbors to flee Baltimore. It also inspired a West Baltimore vigil, which police tried to attend and were promptly threatened by the gathered mourners. This has led the nation at large to believe that the killing was a West Baltimore thing.

The fact is, Scoota spent time on the Eastside and the Westside, and was gunned down on the Eastside, in my neighborhood. As Mescaline Franklin, the recreational photographer who shot the covers of Poet and A Once Great Medieval City, was in town, we

145

decided to go to the liquor store where Scoota died and buy a forty of the local favorite in his honor.

As Mescaline was taking photos of Scoota's memorial—balloons, candles, a stuffed critter, and liquor bottles—that is blocking the sidewalk out front for a week now under the glare of a half dozen Dindus stranded when the #33 overheated and broke down—I spoke to the charming Indian woman whose husband owns the liquor store. After making a purchase I asked her if her building front had been damaged in a car accident and she gave me the narrative in an animated fashion:

"My husband was here, and he is uninjured, although, after the car crashed into the building, the police did not inquire as to his wellbeing. They were only concerned with the famous rapper. The rapper was in his car at the light across the street when the gunman stepped out into the street and shot eleven rounds into the side window and window shield. He tried to drive away but was dead before he hit the building. The police have refused to cooperate with us. I have called over and over again asking for a police report number so that I can file the insurance claim. They refuse, saying it is an open investigation. And then there is the trash shrine out front, it obstructs the walk, the balloons are dangerous to passing cars and I am not about to clean that up. We have been warned not to remove the shrine. The liquor bottles are not even purchased from us, but brought in by the mourners... Thank you so much for asking after our well being—no one else cares. We are alone, behind this counter."

Mescaline and I went outside as the surly Dindus glared at us but made way. One door down is a hipster coffee shop doing brisk business with the pasty patrons from the upscale paleface Waltherson neighborhood directly behind this storefront. The local palefaces do not patronize the liquor store and the Dindus do not use the coffee shop—utter, proximate self-segregation.

Eighteen years ago I stood across the street from this spot, where three young Dindus dealt drugs at the bus stop I used, when they decided to carjack an SUV parked in the very place where Scoota dead-wrecked his ride. The baby that was in the SUV was set out on the sidewalk, eight miles downtown on Hanover Street, as the three businessmen took the vehicle to

Cherry Hill, which is the South Baltimore drug hub where they drew their wholesale product.

Below is one line of Lor Scoota's genius-level poetics, that we have been forever robbed of by that heartless villain who shot him! If you want to hear more, do a YouTube search for Bird Flu by Lor Scoota.

"We sellin' scramble, coke en smack, keep them junkies commin' back."

**Addendum**

As we finish Lor Scoota's forty—Mescaline downing the last drop—my photographer reminded me that the mourning Dindus had written Scoota's epigram on the window of the damaged building, owned by the Hindus! He asked me if there was an ordinance against this and there is. As a supermarket manager, I was routinely reminded by Baltimore City authorities that I had to remove graffiti from the store I managed or pay a fine.

Here's to you, Scoota—shit rolls deep in Dindustan when the Dundids come for you, don't it?

Crackers Cracking Forties by Mescaline Franklin

# Being Jim for an Evening
## Mescaline Franklin in the Evening Land

© 2016 Mescaline Franklin

Jim is working tonight, so I, Mescaline Franklin, am sort of taking his place. He graciously allowed me to house sit his luxury bachelor pad and par take of his selection of fine spirits and reading material. Instead I sat on the porch in the notorious humidity of a Baltimore summer. Observing several of the native inhabitants passing by.

One solidly built, doo-rag sporting fellow walked with what looked like a metal walking cane that was maybe only a foot and half long. Obviously too short to be used for its intended purpose, he held it in the ready and move it slightly up and down in a sort of strange rhythm. He was at least the only pedestrian who did not stare at me as they passed, a few actually greeting me in a neutral manner as I nodded but did not reply.

The mugginess, the clouds in the sky mixed with the slowly descending sun and the surreal and constant background soundtrack of frogs chirping their mating song added to an otherworldly feel that I seem to get

Whenever I visit this place, whatever the season. Literally I am sitting on the edge of what seems like an outpost on an alien world, a settlement in the hostile backwoods of Indian country. After a while I decide to go the twin bars that each represent the two different worlds we muricans have been split up into as plantation subjects. My honor demands I go on foot which I have been advised not to do. There really is no choice for me and I walk down White (boy) Ave, the twilight sky beginning to emerge.

I must admit something, where Mr. LaFond lives is physically beautiful. It is elevated and one can see the skyline of the necropolis to the west quite clearly. The old Episcopal church is downright medieval. The elaborate stone fence that runs along the southwest corner of where Harford Road meets White Avenue has succulents planted in between the spacings evoking a classic European rock garden. The lurid sunset is like that of a dark horror fantasy book cover, menacing yet seductive. As Jonathan Bowden has mentioned, there is something about the gothic and the supernatural that appeals to those of the pale skin in a way that is different than the other races. We are more separated from it yet closer to it at the same time, and able to transcend the veil of it, bringing forth both untold rewards and soul shattering dooms.

I can smell the cooking at the barbeque joint named after the famous predatory nemesis of little red riding hood. This really could be a nice area and I can understand why the hipster homesteaders want to come here. I laugh inside as the progressive policies they push for are making it almost impossible for this to happen.

Unless, somehow, one can get these dindus out to the county. Hmm? Maybe that is their plan, to wait it out and then reap the rising property values? How thoroughly in their class interests yet I do not think they are that clever. You still got a black run city government, yo, and they still don't like or respect you no matter how much you virtue signal to them. What they are trying to divert to their hated working and middle class cousins is going to envelop them as well.

The aforementioned soul shattering dooms are far more devastating to the materialist mind, aka the Lovecraft protagonist aka the hipster SWPL liberal. Well I'm trying to go more in the Robert E. Howard direction thank you very much. That is the key to surviving and thriving in the future, despair being only one kind of fuel and not the end product. The Rudyard Kipling poem of how to be a man is another guide book as is any tome from Mister LaFond.

Well since I was James this evening, I had to act like him. I employed the swivel scan, the deliberate walking pace and the discipline of not talking to anyone outdoors in any capacity. I look like a macho asshole without trying to and disturbingly like many of the heroin addicts walking around with their two hour sleep patterns. I must focus on my goal, watering hole A and then watering hole B.

Watering hole A has some kind of trivia game going on and I recognize Quinn who is a friendly patron Jim and I have had many a conversation with. We fist bump and talk a bit. I get a Natty Boh' on draft and find the trivia to actually be quite literary in nature with questions about Emily Dickinson and Tennyson poems. Whoa, even I don't know that shit.

I sit in the empty area where I believe a drug deal is going down and I am being observed but not intimidated. I am that weird out of town tattooed smiling guy they have seen before with "Santa Claus", writing down ideas on a napkin with my pilot pen and harmless. Being weird is another form of protection I have found so fly the freak flag as they say.

I leave and then cross Harford Road to watering hole B, the hipster spot. The bartender looks like a lesbian but she seems to really like me and is perhaps bisexual. I notice a tattoo on her ear as she gets me a local saison beer. I sit near the window and look as the sky is now darker but with a bit of light left. The abendlandes. The West. In the space of a half hour I count three separate groups of youths walking by, all in threes. Interesting.

As I leave in the increasing darkness, the only group I notice are two shirtless white trash dudes walking across the street in the same direction. White nationalist I may be I know these men are not my brothers and I listen to them talk loudly to each other. Pathetic and degenerate as they may be I keep them in my peripheral.

I pass the BBQ place and decide to get the special; a wonderful combination of bacon, brisket and pulled pork with a sweet sauce. Now there is something worth defending even more than myself! Nothing on this shadow world is going to stop me from eating this thing with a can of beer in the bachelor pad. Turning onto White Avenue, the fourth group of youngsters is coming in the opposite direction. They are walking in the street like me. I see acknowledge them with a nod and keep my pace, they eye me back but keep walking.

The aptly named White Avenue has its namesake denizens sitting on their porches, halfway hidden, smoking, talking, drinking but not venturing beyond their yard or driveway. They look at me probably figuring I am one of the half way house guys. I reach the LaFond estate and decide to hang on the porch as well. The frog's mating song was now at a crescendo and I did not want to go inside. Give me the night, as the old George Benson song goes.

I should be enraged by this scenario and in the day time, when more lucid thoughts and reason hold sway, I am.

The people that rule us encourage this low scale war on us. You give them your money, sweat and they now want your blood or at the very least (and more likely) do not give a damn if its spilled.

But the twilight sky and darkness has a magic, the subtle dread being the flip side of an indescribable ecstasy Having the waitress at watering hole B up in the bachelor pad would have been the perfect punctuation to wandering around the Evening Land. There is a meaning, even in this empty waste land of modernity. Just because we only know a heap of broken images, as Eliot said, we can indeed "know" if we only feel the primal within us and link it to the energies ever flowing around us.

This is how things should be. The real world is coming back, kamerads. The question of out time is: can the Hollow Men be filled again?

And with what?

I have an idea. Read on brothers.

# If Trump Wins
## Will He Be Killed, Marginalized or Effective?

© 2016 James LaFond

Our reader of record, Sam J., has recently commented to this old crackpot that "Trump will crush Hillary!"

My first thought was, "Maybe so, but he better be wary of the reach around—the Wicked Witch of the Left surely has lethal vampire claws and an arm that dislocates at the elbow and turns into a mining tool of S&M sorts."

Sam, I would like to make you an offer—a bet of sorts, as I am confident that the next master of this plantation will by strapping on, not unzipping, to do your nation wrong behind closed doors:

If your toupee-crowned savior gets in, I will send you two PDFs of your choice.

If Trump gets in, recall that not a person working for the Federal government will have voted for him, and try not to act surprised when the CIA kills him, while his Secret Service Detail looks the other way and the FBI covers it up and blames it on one of Jared Taylor's American Renaissance readers. In such a case, I'll send you a copy of When You're Food: Raw.

If the Queen Aspirant is victorious, then I will send you four PDFs of your choice—might I suggest some dark fantasy and horror to set the matriarchal mood...

**Reader Poll**

While we are at it, lets take a reader poll and if you win, be sure and write in and remind me so that I can send out the literary missivepiece of your choice:

If Trump wins:

1. Will he be assassinated?

2. Will he simply be marginalized by the media and congress?

3. Or, might he prove effective in reversing [to any degree] the ongoing discount sale of America?

I think he will be murdered, and what is more, the media and both political parties will blame him and claim that he not only brought this on himself, but so damaged the American faith in their government, that the government will need to be strengthened to reverse the damage and heal the gaping multicultural wound left by his unbridled hatred.

And remember, Paleface, before you cast your vote, it is Dawn in Dindustan!

# Black Terminatrix Outfitter
## BT-1000 Bestiary: The Latest Full Line from Cyberdine Systems

© 2016 James LaFond

*Please, if you know Tommy, send him a link to this for his own use.*

YouTube commentator, Tommy Sotomayor discovered a few years back that The Terminator movies were in fact a cover for a real Skynet cybernetics program, that, rather than take over the world for a self-aware computer network, serves the function of emasculating African American men and producing violet mobs of urban youth aggressive enough to terrorize civilians but with enough "bitch in the blood" from being "bitch-raised," instead of fathered, to prevent them from becoming a real threat to the government.

Since Tommy is not a social scientist he has tended to use the most abundant model of Black Terminatrix or "BT-1000" as shorthand for the entire cybernetic catalog and has also used various model numbers with a modicum of accuracy. So, in the interest of Science, we, at the National Institute for the Study of the Dinduological Arts, have commissioned Webone Shoop, renowned [in East Baltimore] Dinduologist, to make sense of this admittedly confusing variety of BT units.

So, Professor Shoop, how does one define the BT-1000 and other models?

"Jungle Jim, you might be a cracker, but at least you know how to admit when your conniving kind had the demise of my kind in mind. The fact is, Crackerkind invented the BT-1000 when y'all started paying our women to kick our asses to the curb as soon as they drop a baby. So it is not a factor of these bitches being built—or even being machines—but of their minds being reprogrammed with advertising, which is amplified by the possession of an EBT card, kind of like a signal amplifier and the signal goes off when they are first impregnated, which gets you the following Cybedine upgrade table. The dates are not date of birth, but date of transmogrification, which happens at impregnation. Hell, the bitch will be whooping yo ass and it won't make no sense as she always been a sweet little shorty up until then, then here comes the baby bump...

BT-800, activated from 1965-80

BT-900, activated from 1981-95

BT-1000, activated from 1996-2006

BT-1100, activated from 2006-2014

BT-1200, activated from 2015-2200

"As you can see, activation rates are increasing as shelf-life decreases, making for a volatile mix.

"Oh yes, if you rich crackers still want to continue sending these bitches to destroy black culture in urban and suburban America, by all means go to the cybernetic salon and get your wigs, hair-extensions, seven-inch hooped earrings, Vietnamese fingernails and gold teeth!"

## Tommy's Bestie Channel

https://www.youtube.com/user/TommysEpicRants3

# The Dindu Next Door
## Dare Go Da Naybarhood

Edward lives in an upscale middle-class enclave in Baltimore County, which has luckily been missed by the Government's Dindu resettlement initiative. However, a couple of the folks in this suburban brownstone neighborhood have lost their houses, which have been flipped and rented to welfare families from the city. One such family lives on Edward's block. They are polite, wave, the mother making her kids stay off Edward's property, but you might be able to take the Dindu out of Dindumore but not Dindumore out of his soul.

"You see that shopping cart at the end of the alley, where it meets the street, right next to my neighbor's garden, how it is all full of trash and compost?

"Well, they rolled their groceries home in that cart, then used the card to clean up the yard for the 4th of July picnic and rolled it to the end of the alley and flipped it over. Who does that?"

I responded, "Oh, your neighbor dindu nuffin! It's your fault for not hiring them a landscaper and paying to have their free groceries delivered."

Edward looked skyward as if trying to conjure up an understanding deity and sighed, "I suppose I'll call the supermarket and have them come get it."

Generally, the first signs of Dindu occupancy are:

1. Double parking or walking in the middle of the street depending in whether or not they are motorists or pedestrians

2. Drink containers left on the curb and in the street next to where they clean out their parked cars.

3. Lookouts on perpetual duty on rental porches.

## Naziphobea
### The Chief Dindu Psychological Affliction

Last night, when I got into work near to 1 a.m., I walked by Carl—a young, anachronistic hippie—who Tyrice was whining to, about the trials and tribulations of being a Dindu victim of white racism and police harassment.

I looked at them directly—which is taboo among the young manginas of Dindustan. Carl grinned as Tyrice looked at me with open fear, afraid I might speak. I looked at them questioningly and Carl said that some brothers in Dallas had gunned down some cops.

I looked at Tyrice and said, "Two weeks ago I had a cunt pig screaming at me down in the city with her hand on her gun, for the crime of being a white pedestrian. The more cops get killed the more cops

166

freak out and go for their gun under stress. I'll probably be shot by a pig long before the hoodrats get me."

Carl shook his head as Tyrice cringed in horror, staring at my shaven head as if I were the king of all racist, Dindu-nerd-eating bikers. The other Dindu coworkers would not even talk to me last night, for, in their highly conditioned, media enthralled, suburban world, any white man who is not terrified of Dindus on sight—and most are—is a mass murdering race warrior. However, this is only partially racially-sensitive conditioning. The greater part of the problem—a problem because it does absolutely prohibit communication between them and I, and I represent one of their few chances at gathering useful information about re-growing the ball sack that their mothers clipped off at birth—is emasculation. When young men are physically incapable of making eye contact with an older man that is not physically imposing, loud or aggressive—as arc all the young men under 24 of bother races I work with—then there is no person-to-person exchange of information and their generation stays locked into the media loop, eating, drinking and breathing The Everlasting Lie.

The only thing required to destroy a culture is emasculation. The frantic and deep-seated Dindu fears of whites and of any white leader that does not wallow in racial guilt, is essentially rooted in widespread emasculation.

Just how do we re-grow balls on a steer?

# The Caliph of Dindustan
### The Crackpot Case for the Dindu-and-Chief

© 2016 James LaFond

This morning, at about 5 a.m., Butch called me, told me that about ten cops had been shot down in Dallas by Dindus, and was then outraged that the president was not doing his job of unifying the American people. Butch just wanted to vent, so I tried to sooth his nerves:

"Butch, your leader—my warden—*is* doing his job. His job *is* to divide the American people."

A stream of expletives poured over the air ways. When he caught his breath, I assured him that his Caliph was adhering to the Faith:

"Butch, when a nation is on the rise a head-of-state who unifies the state's social components toward the same goal, is desirable. However a state in decline must be served by a figurehead who knows how to— and acts on this knowledge—to keep the various classes, races and faiths at each other's throats in order to preserve the hegemony of his class/race/faith."

I would like to be able to say I heard the click of his phone snapping shut, but it was just the deafening sound of silence that brought serenity back to my morning.

## Dindu Cosmology
### Why Dindus Have More of a Clue Than You

© 2016 James LaFond

Palefaces, complacent in their shuddering masses, as the Lie they were fed for generations has blossomed into quite a different felonious flower than they were led to believe, seem to be confused and in disagreement as to why Dindus do what they do.

I see the dichotomy between the secularly pale and objectively frail as cosmological in nature.

Palefaces have been indoctrinated for generations into the belief that they are free and that their leaders were mere public service providers. They get upset when this dubious social contract remains unfulfilled and will soon be persuasively brought to heel with little overt effort. Indeed, they will beg to be brought into the utopian fold because of constant Dindu violence.

171

Dindus are the perfect threat to hold over the heads of the cowardly paleface middleclass, for, as their self-descriptive moniker states, they "Dindu nuffin." Where a human being of most types would insist that they have agency, that they elevate presidents, bring prosperity to such struggling concerns as Wal-Mart and Pepsico, the Dindu sees clearly his reality, and knows, immediately, that he was only following directions, that he is a mere moral mule who does his master's bidding.

Many Dindu adults who decried the Baltimore riots and purge of a year ago are no supportive of the outburst as they have been told that a white person attending the Baltimore Orioles game on the first night of unrest used the N-word! Imagine belonging to a group of people that must mindlessly engage in mob violence at the single utterance of a word of power by a member of the master race? Imagine how frantic your every day would be, how agitated you would be, if the world had conspired to rob you of self-discipline at the chemical level?

Your belief in such things as Freedom and Democracy offer little succor to the contemplative mind in this world of enthrallment and oligarchy. But the Dindu is a willing thrall, who knows purpose, patronage and peace-of-mind, born of the deep-seated knowledge that in the end, it is always some other person's problem.

# Jesse!
## Congratulations, Brother

© 2016 James LaFond

For your generous contribution, we, at The National Center for the Study of the Dinduological Arts, have arranged for an all expenses paid for you, by you, tour of Lesser Dindustan. A tent will be pitched at the park across the street from the Baltimore County 8th Precinct building. Along with this authentic tent you will be issued a bugle to summon the police posted at the front desk, and a battery of replica Congreve rockets left over from the 4th of July.

When you are attacked by the Dindoo mutineers we expect a stiff upper lip, a steely eye and no quarter given to those beastly savages! Unfortunately, though we seem to be out of maxim guns... Never fear, Old Boy, your faithless guide shall be none other than Webone Shoop.

# The White Stranger
## Melissa and Tammy in Dindustan

© 2016 James LaFond

Early July, 2016, 2:20 p.m., Parkville, Baltimore County, Maryland

Melissa and Tammy were walking across White Oak toward Loch Raven Boulevard to get a snowball at the stand in front of the 7-11 when there was a shout.

"White girl!" came from behind them as four Dindu breeders, in that agitated state just before being fertilized with their first Dindu hatchling, walked hard to overtake them, repeating, "White girl!"

Melissa shielded Tammy, who was small and petite, as the four Dindu breeders—being joined by two Dindu fertilizer drones who were crossing the street—fanned out threateningly, jutting out their jaws and glaring as their leader said, "Give it up, white girl," as she pointed at Tammy's smart phone.

At that moment an evil shadow was cast upon the bucolic scene, when a vile oppressor, a bald, bearded, white man, who for some insane reason—obviously his ass was insane yo!—did not quiver in fear at the sight of Dindu aggression. This cruel interloper, utterly failing to respect the centuries of suffering endured by these innocent Dindus, inflicted on them by people who looked vaguely like Tammy and Melissa, appeared to be walking to his car from an adjacent house, but stopped behind Melissa and Tammy and looked calmly at the assembled Dindu dignitaries.

With a shudder, Melissa and Tammy bunched together, fearing that this evil man might do something that could get them in even more Dindu trouble. However, neither he nor the Dindus advanced—nor did he continue to his car, but simply stood, silently, with keys in hand, smiling at the two fertilizer drones, who nodded to him, to each other, and then said to the lead Dindu breeder, "Yo, lez go."

With a hard swallow and a jerky nod of her well-coifed head, the lead breeder and her three raider-maids

176

reluctantly gave up their quest for Justice—a winged angel of righteous retribution yet barely fluttering beyond their reach—turned on their heels and began walking back east, in the direction they had come, shadowed by their two fertilizer drones who kept to the street, walking just off the curb in their escort role.

Melissa and Tammy looked at the man, looked at each other, and became fearful of his intentions and hurried on past him, having learned the salient lesson that sometimes, in Dindustan, one evil might save a victim from another evil. The fact that the stranger had looked directly into the eye of an apex predator in their world and had not backed down, obviously meant he was a serial killer—a rapist at least! They picked up their pace and walked as quickly as they could to the snowball stand as the creepy man got into his car and followed them, looking at them while he idled at the traffic light, and not leaving them alone until they were finally sheltered under the protective umbrella of the snowball stand.

## The Taboo Masculine

I did not interview Melissa and Tammy, and in fact made their names up. One is a small, tanned, blonde girl, the other a slightly overweight brunette. The account was had from a motorist that witnessed what he thought was a crime in progress and then kept an eye on the situation until the people he perceived as the targets of a violent crime appeared to be safe among adults of their own kind. The entire time he was conscious of the apparent fear the two white girls had for him and surmised that they had been raised by single mothers who had coached their girls on the evil attentions of men. He felt somewhat sickened by the experience of being so feared by the girls—that they regarded him more fearfully then the male aggressors did, and the fact that the female aggressors had no fear of him, but seemed to simply acknowledge him as a temporary obstacle to achieving their goals— put him in a kind of "culture shock."

In a real society, in an intact culture, this man would have felt morally justified in speaking with the parents of the girls, at the very least. But in a world where every white man is a rapist or serial killer, this is not possible. It is significant that no TV show or movie made since 2008 [find one and put the link in the comments section below] would depict the hunters in this situation as an aggressor type, but that weekly TV shows and most movies constantly bombard

Americans with the message that white men abduct, rape and kill white women and girls at epidemic levels, when, in fact, the overriding instinct among all American men that I have worked and trained with is to protect all women from aggression.

TV and movies provide the postmodern mythology that was once provided by myth, religion and ethnic iconography, informing the perception of our fellow citizens. It is bizarre that our current myth of the ravaging, multi-murdering, rapist white man is so vastly divergent from the reality as to make casual aid between strangers living in close proximity into a threat. In the current climate, any woman who would have [probably with much verbiage] done the same thing this man did would have been hailed as a media hero for a three minute news segment, where he was immediately feared by those he had casually aided.

Masculine myth makers, including the poets of ancient times and the adventure writers I grew up reading, such as Edgar Rice Burroughs, Robert E. Howard and Louis L'Amour, traditionally sketch a set of behavioral expectations for young men to emulate. In our current society, such mythmaking has now been in the hands of women and emasculated males of a docile, handwringing type for over a generation. Such mythmakers glory in the parasitic metaphor of the vampire and the parasitic actuality of the law enforcer and politician to arrive at a scolding form of mythology that excuses complaisance and denies the free will so exemplified by the heroes of legend, history and fiction that once informed a masculine mythos that supported human culture.

The story of Melissa and Tammy and The White Stranger exposes 21st Century America as an anti-heroic society, a society which Robert E. Howard, preeminent author of heroic pulp fiction [1926-36] predicted in his story, Vulture's Roost, unsold in his life time. In this taut, western adventure, the female lead in the story rushes to the aid of a back-shooting criminal who is being beaten by a working man he tried to murder. Taking the murdering criminal's side and regarding the hyper-masculine working man as a monster out of some monstrous age, the law-abiding woman aligns herself with the emasculated criminal. That story echoed like a great bell in this reader's mind as he read it in a gym two blocks from the scene of The White Stranger, in a municipality currently being overrun by state-sanctioned, media-supported aggression of the meanest type, in a world where training men to fight—the ancient currency of heroes—has accounted for a greater portion of my pariah status than my anti-authoritarian beliefs.

It is a certainty that a tribe without heroes is dead, and that a culture without internal cohesion is doomed. But a society in which mutual aid is taboo and masculinity itself is a clear sign of evil intent, a society in which heroic status is granted to passive victims and in which real men are an object of deepest distrust, what kind of society is that?

## 'Upside Down'
### Thirty Seconds with Arvin

© 2016 James LaFond

I just returned from the ghetto mart with discount humus and avocado meant for the food service industry and club retailers that Ghetto Ed gets ahold of via an overrun contract with a food wholesaler. If they make too much, Ed get's to make a bid.

On the way out the door, just before lifting my bag from the register back, I noticed Arvin, who I have not spoken with since his fellow security guard, who worked across the street until a few weeks ago, was murdered by masked hoodlums. Arvin is a young black fellow with shaven head, a good build for a middleweight boxer and a polite smile that is none too easy. His carriage is a mixture of vigilance and fright, grace and despair as he stands with his back to the ice machine looking around, his head on a swivel, armed only with a badge.

I stepped up to Arvin and asked, "Do you need me to go get Ed?" figuring this was a "bigass shoplifter" situation in the mid-stages of development.

He looked at me and said, "No, nothin' he can do that he ain't did. The world's upside down. Last week we had this brother in here saying we had too many whites working here and he was going to blow the place up, burn it down, kill everybody. Ed called the cops. The cops talked to the dude. The dude left spouting hate and dead promises. The cops apologized, said that they can't arrest on threats anymore, that they got ta talk that shit out, that if they ain't no gun, ain't no knife, ain't no body, that it's all good."

I looked at him and nodded, tipped my hat to him and said, "Keep your back to the ice machine," and walked out into the suffocating July heat.

It's not "all good" in the hood.

## Miss Mary Ellen
**Crossing the Street with A Harm City Historian**

© 2016 James LaFond

Miss Mary Ellen was waiting for traffic to slow so she could shuffle across the street with her two light grocery bags, cane and keys, a bag on each gloved wrist, her pale skin protected by her broad straw hat, her sky blue dress putting the overcast sky to shame. I had some place to be and didn't have an hour to walk her home at her considered pace, but did have a solid minute to help her across those two lanes by waltzing slowly next to her as I threatened fenders with my recently acquired Santa Clause bulk, where Miss Mary Ellen would be lucky to scratch their paint at about 80 pounds.

Knowing of my avocation she asked me of things violent, about how things have gotten out in the suburbs she never consented to migrate to with her fleeing family.

"Violence is the same in the City as this time last year, with assault, threat and verbal aggression up, and new, out of state, middleclass, white home buyers up as well. But in the County, its gone from suburbia to outer hood over the past 10 months, like a crime plague. It's ridiculous. the County cops are overwhelmed and falsifying the stats, misreporting crimes, not reporting crimes, etc.

Miss Mary Ellen shook her Head, paused in traffic to look at me and then began to speak as we continued across the right lane, "My mother saw the flu of 1918. She was a seamstress—worked for the rich. When they sent the Gold Teeth after us and sent the men to war, she said that this is how it would be, a changaroo; the Gold Teeth driving us out of the city, then once we were all out there, the Gold Teeth would come again and the rich would take back the city—the old changaroo. That is why we never moved, Mom and me, but the kids and the cousins, they all went and the Gold Teeth are coming for them, aren't they?"

Up on the curb now, in front of the snowball stand and hair salon, I wished Miss Mary Ellen a good day, and walked off, wondering that what a seamstress had known would come to pass had been overlooked as history looked the other way.

# Rosalie

## An Authentic Baltimore Icon on Back Alley Zumba, Dindu Academia and the Blooming Race War

© 2016 James LaFond

*Rosalie is a Northeast Baltimore original, a retired math teacher and the former hostess of an authentic Italian restaurant, which closed not long ago because of Dindus robbing patrons out front. She was once a customer of mine when I was a supermarket manager. I ran into her today in front of the Fenwick Bakery in Parkville on the City side of the line. With some Baltimoreans you only need to ask them how they are doing and you get an earful, in public, as the Dindus walk by, giving her "you can't say that" looks.*

Enjoying the race war, darling. You know we live in a communist country. People think I'm crazy when I say that. But we are being made to do everything we don't want to do and have everything done to us by the people that are above the law. I was going to get back into teaching but they don't want white teachers anymore, not even out in the county. Everything is going black. My grandchild is only one of eleven white children in the entire school and he gets attacked by these little shits every day. My baby goes to school to learn, because it's the law, and these turds with arms and legs swarm him like flies swarm on them. Of course the teacher looks the other way. What's she going to do, go against her own?

You know the Bel Loc Diner is closing. It's going to be a Starbucks. Not in time though. Last year my niece was beaten to death in the alley by niggers, right behind the diner. I'll die by a nigger hand too, because I'm not backing down from these fucking animals.

Last night, in the alley behind my daughter's house—I live with my daughter now to help with the children— we have these so-called upscale middleclass blacks, four pretty coons with their hooped earrings and fake braids all the way down to their asses, reciting a Zumba performance in the alley. I shit you not, baby. These bitches had a fucking PA system hooked up in the alley! I was gardening because it was still light out, had my shovel. But the baby was sleeping. There is no speaking to these people. So my daughter calls the police and a cop comes. He is standing their telling her he can't do a thing even though it's against the noise ordinance. If they don't want to move he can't move them. He's not supposed to lock anybody up, just speak to them, mediation.

Now, the entire time the cop is talking to my daughter, these whores are threatening her for calling the cops, so I flip them the finger. Then they start complaining to the cop that I flipped them the finger. He asked me if I did, so I asked the leader bitch what finger I flipped her, and she said, "The middle finger."

I said, "Congratulations, that's the third finger. I didn't think you could count that high."

So she says, "Oh, you a smart bitch, huh? Well, you a fat bitch too. You oughta be taken our Zumba."

Oh, I knew I had her then, thought maybe she'd come across the alley at me. I said, "No, Baby Girl, I get enough exercise riding your husband's big black cock for eight hours a day while you're at work. It's awful nice of you to let him stay home to take care of Old Rosalie!"

*[Hysterical laughter as a bystander looks on with fear as Rosalie gestures expressively, her eyes widening, her volume climbing.]*

Let me tell ya, baby, that tweety-bird bitch was ready to bring it, started across the alley swinging her braids so you could hear them slap on that hard monkey ass of hers. Well, the cop is holding her back and the other bitch is eye-balling me, so I tell her, "Come on, I'll bury your ass with this shovel, bitch!"

She starts telling the cop, "She threaten me, officer, she threaten me!"

Of course, the cop is stupid, but he's not a complete idiot, and did overhear me say something, so he turns to me and says, "What did I hear you say, Miss?"

I turned on the Rosalie charm, batted my eye lashes at him and said, "Oh, excuse me for interrupting, Officer Handsome, but I was just saying to my neighbor that "Burying this grass with this shovel is a bitch.""

Baby, I don't say shit around a cop unless I have an alternate version. Those whores were fit to be tied. My daughter and girlfriend keep getting on me about back-talking the niggers, but I like black people, so it's pretty damned hard for me to put up with niggers. I'm standing my ground. On my tombstone it 'ill read, "Here lies Rosalie, killed for back-talking niggers."

*I understand that people will have a variety of opinions on Rosalie, and she would understand as well—and tell you exactly where your opinion belongs. But what struck me the most about this story—told on a sidewalk while pedestrians gave us a wide berth—was how much it must suck to be a Baltimore City Police officer! Look, I hate pigs as much as the next irascible misanthrope, but I have to pity any cop that has to referee such altercations. After a few years of this kind of action I think I'd be primed to shoot first and ask questions later.*

*Note: there is no truth to the rumor that Rosalie was the inspiration for the AC-DC song "Whole Lot a Rosie." The song was inspired by a Baltimore woman, who I also knew, but briefly, who was a stripper, not a teacher-hostess.*

# Running Up The Flag
## Dindu Annexation and Occupation News

© 2016 James LaFond

The following is a summary from the front lines in East Dindustan.

**Baltimore City**

Numerous shooting of Dindus by Dundids have occurred in front of officers of the BPD.

Saint Dominic's Church in Hamilton is under siege. The old paleface ladies attending mass are being bum-rushed, strong armed and pushed down by Dindu purse collectors. The pastor has recommended that parishiners not carry purses to church.

Paleface homeowners have been displaying and flying multiple American flags as they bar their side

192

windows and doors, even as record numbers of their neighbors put their houses up for sale.

## Parkville, White Marsh, Rosedale Precincts of Baltimore County

The East County Times, which covers these precincts, has stopped publishing a police blotter, retitled it as Crime Trends, featuring misrepresented underreporting of general trends in Parkville, news of a murder suspect charged in Essex and man found beaten nearly to death in Dundalk. However, it is known by this reporter that violent crime is continuing to climb in these precincts, with, especially in Rosedale and White Marsh, where their have been five mob attacks, two knife robberies and three stickups over the past week, all Dindu on paleface. This is only news from personal friends and must be considered a tiny sample.

Parkville residents are posting record numbers of for sale signs it looks like 15% based on my crude survey], with multiple flag displays apparent on many houses that are not for sale. There has never been such a display of American flags—even on Memorial Day and

Independence Day—in my memory. No houses, in or out of the city, that are for sale, also fly a flag.

Is there a national conservative initiative that I am not aware of?

## Essex Precinct

The Avenue News has reported five knife attacks in Essex [two being mob attacks], two unarmed mob attacks and three "lone dawg" Dindu attacks, all are Dindu on paleface, except for one Dundid on Dindu attack.

The crime spread is broader than ever in all areas of Baltimore City and Baltimore County, with the County experiencing a huge surge in violent crime [mostly unreported] and auto-theft, with burglary staying about the same. I do not know the reason behind the flag displays, but suspect that the paleface targets of the Dindu insurgency are hoping to illicit police sympathy for their cause or might be showing support for the recently slain officers across Dindustan.

# A Whore Moment
## A book you really need with Dindustan on the rise

© 2016 James LaFond

I have never seriously tried to sell anything I've written. The idea of hawking my own books is unseemly at best. However, with the recent trends I am seeing, 14-month post riot trends in Baltimore and Baltimore County, that are far worse than being reported, far worse than I thought they would be, expecting another riot as I was. I would have been attacked a dozen times over in as many months if I did not practice what I preach in Thriving in Bad Places. The Media State has made its play and is busily discrediting its own police so that they can be replaced by police who are not of the same race as the target population. White cops are DOJ and Dindu targets so that they might be replaced by corrupt cops from Dindu and Alien populations—which is well underway in New York as I write. [I have an inside Gotham Pig source.]

Within the next ten years, if you live in any American city or suburb, you will not be able to defend yourself with the necessary force to deal with a Dindu pack without facing Dindu cops. There will also be practical limits on where you can move. How many small rural towns need your skill set? Many of my readers are going to be stuck in Dindustan as it wells up around them, as it appears next door just after you move in...

Thriving in Bad Places is all about observing and negotiating such an environment without resorting to the means that will bring the Dindustani Police Farce down on you as the Media adhans call for your livelihood and remaining social autonomy to be offered up on the Altar of their Ape God.

Do your self a favor and get a copy of this book.

If you are strictly an e-reader, it won't be out on kindle until August.

# The Muddy Gut Hive

## Dinduography #1: Leaving the Bar and Hungry in Dindustan?—Don't Do It Son!

© 2016 James LaFond

At one in the morning, in the suburban shit cave known as Essex, Maryland, where Dindu hordes have recently migrated in overwhelming numbers, four blocks from where I off load from the #55 bus at the Aldis on the corner of Old Eastern Avenue, on a recent Saturday night, a man leaving Jad's Caddy Shack—an eatery with bar—was attacked. He may have been an employee based on the late hour.

## Dinduography Timeout

Now, reader, please go to the link below and view the map.

https://www.bing.com/mapspreview?&ty=18&q=Jad
%27s%20Caddy%20Shack%20Essex%20MD&ss=ypi
d.YN873x16956909039650817954&ppois=39.30990
98205566_-
76.4453277587891_Jad%27s%20Caddy%20Shack_Y
N873x16956909039650817954~&cp=39.30991~-
76.445328&v=2&sV=1

Follow Williams Road south. Now grab the map and drag south as you cross Southeast Boulevard [I. Ext. 702] on Williams Road. There is a covered—completely encased in steel mesh—footbridge over this Interstate Extension 702. Now drag down across the highway to the warren of short arching streets. 10,000 Dindus live here—a hoodrat hive! Drag the map around to describe the line of the peninsula and you will see a veritable containment camp for Dindus, bordered by Deep Creek on the left and Muddy Gut—I shit you not!—on the right. The two vectors for crime are Back River Neck and Marlyn, which both cross Eastern Avenue and Old Eastern. That stretch of Eastern-Old Eastern is a nightmare hunting zone, with daylight home invasions and worse. The 702 extension is the route used by motorist of the upscale and red neck variety that live and recreate on Turkey

Point, Holly Neck, Brown's Creek, Rocky Point, Sue Creek and Middle River.

The Dindu drones, in order to win breeding rights with the queens, must walk across the footbridge—where they are sadly prevented from bricking paleface motorists below by the dastardly steel mesh—and hunt along Back River Neck Road and Old Eastern Avenue. The Marlyn Avenue route serves more as a drug supply conduit, with Middleborough and Hyde park the distribution hub. This is what happens when liberals decide to colonize waterfront suburbs on a peninsula; you get gauntlet predation from the [DH] Dindu hive, positioned between a [PWR] paleface, waterfront refuge and the [IMIZ] inland mixed interaction zone.

## Ambush

On the parking lot of Jad's Caddyshack, this man ran straight into a semicircle of Dindus, who hit him, knocked him down, beat him and stabbed him. He is recovering well, never saw the knife, did not recognize the "unknown suspects," who, of course Dindu Nuffin! He does not seem to have been robbed. Any place at which you eat or drink after dark is an ambush zone, as Dindu hordlings prefer well-fed prey.

## Ambush Notes

Late night carry outs are prime stakeout zones, where Dindus ambush the soon to be did for the crime of wanting a club sandwich after leaving the bar. This is a far more reliable way to hit the alcohol-impaired adult on his way to his lair than at the bar. For the bars these adults exit, often have cigarette smokers as lookouts. The best thing about forcing cigarette smokers outside, in Maryland, has been that so many bar patrons are out front smoking at a given time, that Dindus no longer ambush on the lot or in front of the bar, but observe the bar traffic from afar and stakeout the eateries and gas stations where patrons will stop on their way home. Now, Jad's profiles primarily as an eatery, not a bar, with little or no smoking outside. It would be safer to take food from Jad's just before dark, and then go eat it at a bar or at home.

Get your gas before you go to the bar.

Patronize a bar that serves food, or get your carryout and take it to the bar and eat there, like we do at the mixed race sports bar in Hamilton, where everyone stopping for a sub or pizza after leaving the bar has been marked and attacked by the Dindu Hitta Youth from their observation posts, which the police permit them to maintain.

If you work at a place like Jad's, you cannot leave alone or unarmed. The most solid fact the Dindus will learn is when you leave, especially since they will have a dishwasher or line cook [after your boss or you fires them for smoking dope behind the dumpster] giving intelligence from the inside. You should have a driver or footman [I do this] waiting outside for the half hour leading up to your exit. A developing Dindu pack may be spotted from his vantage, provided he does not position himself by the door, which is stupid. He needs to stand off and then meet you at the door, staying in cell phone contact so he can warn you to stay locked down if a pack has gathered.

Ultimately, even at a location that types as mid-risk, like Jad's, proximity to large numbers of Dindus makes it dangerous. This has happened to Valentino's in my neighborhood, a popular eatery for Dindus who like high fat food, and therefore have eyes on the establishment for potential targets. The Dindu's have virtually claimed the area around Valentino's to the point where it no longer serves as a bus transfer point after dark.

## The Other End of the Bus Line

Below is the Baltimore City high crime eatery location at the head of my bus trip that takes me to within four blocks of Jads. I pick up the bus a few blocks down Northern Parkway, within sight of this intersection, but will only use this stop in heavy rain or snow. Recently, since the 2015 Purge, crime at this city transfer point has gotten worse, and at the county transfer point at the Aldis, it has gotten much worse, meaning that both locations are now equally dangerous at night, with the difference being that since the Aldi's stop is a half mile from a County police station, you will never, ever see a cop there, unlike the Valentino's location, where cops patrol by in their car regularly, but have been unable to prevent the Valentino Crew from gathering in strength and dominating the corner. The pigs have, instead, opted to harass and arrest lone white males in the area, including myself a few weeks ago, when a cunt pig screamed at me—after a skulking Dindu called on me for committing the racist crime of making eye contact with him and standing my ground—apparently unmindful of the fact that her hand had strayed to her gun.

http://www.bing.com/search?q=valentinos+restaurant&form=CPDTDF&pc=EUPP_CPDTDF&src=IE-SearchBox

https://www.bing.com/mapspreview?&ty=18&q=Valentino%27s%20Restaurant%20Baltimore%20MD&ss=ypid.YN405x58605737&ppois=39.3630905151367_-76.5519027709961_Valentino%27s%20Restaurant_YN405x58605737~&cp=39.363091~-76.551903&v=2

## The Dindustan Library
**A Harm City Librarian Flees the Baltimore Race Purge only to End Up in another East Coast Morality Pit**

© 2016 James LaFond

Ajay, a fine Southern lady of color, with a master's degree in library science, and also my former roommate, fled Baltimore this time last year in the wake of the riots and the ongoing purge. Her rental was on the battlefront and she could not stand having the BPD chopper over her flat, pouring its spotlight in through her curtained window as hoodrats fled the popo past her condo. What was worse, was her job as a Baltimore City librarian was closer to being an adult daycare operator than to anything she had spent a lifetime in school for, such as being the caretaker of a portion of humanity's brain trust.

I cannot reveal the East Dindustan City Ajay landed a job in, only to say that it is not nearly as bad a place as Baltimore, and that it has been targeted for ghettoization, which has put her, as a librarian, on the front line. Here she goes with a brief summary of her job description as assistant branch manager, in her new hometown, which I shall call Yotopia.

"It is not as dangerous as Baltimore. The people are not as violent—thank God. Yotopia is simultaneously being re-gentrified and importing addicts. My facility is part of a "new look initiative" for the city and we are busy making it look presentable for the rich white people. The crazy thing about a public library is that we have two kinds of patrons, the literate old money and the illiterate poor.

"The specific problem in Baltimore was teenage hoodlums whose mothers dropped them off as a free, unscheduled day care appointment, and who would then come back and threaten to beat you up—even fight the police—if you put their child out for disturbing the environment with their fist fights, pornography, rap music and obnoxious, loud swearing.

"At least here I have an on-duty uniformed police officer rather than a worthless rent-a-cop. But it would be nice if we had experienced cops. Unfortunately, they assign graduating cadets to the library as a training post. In that respect I am acting as a police training officer, as I am supposed to take the lead with interactions—the light touch policy. The Board of Directors does not want Mrs. Isenberg to have her reading of the latest novel disturbed by Officer So-in-so beating the shit out a homeless addict, or some welfare mamma arguing about her inalienable right to house her noxious—never-should-have-been-hatched—brood in the public library.

"You would love my boss. She does not know her job and depends on me for all necessary library science matters, as well as for actually abiding by policy in maintaining the facility, which is the major portion of the job. She's milk chocolate, pretty, plenty of firm boobage, a small waste and plenty of butt—all jammed into something too damned tight for business casual, perfect for breeding an offensive backfield, I suppose. She told me straight up that I was running the place while she wrote her first novel. She even has me go into her wallet and get her card and make bank trips for her. She calls me "Goodie-goodie," I suppose because I'm the first black person she has known who hasn't stolen from her. It's like she's a queen and I'm her handmaiden, totally unprofessional on her end, with a swear word emerging from her mouth at least once in every sentence.

"So, while she's writing the great American novel, I'm supervising the cleaning of homeless urine and feces and the resulting stains, off of the walls and sidewalks of the building, trimming back the bushes so that they cannot be used for primate nesting. Some organization is using the Trailways bus company to ship busloads of these homeless people and drug addicts to the gas station across the street. The bus line simply ends at the gas station! Maybe it is some other, more far gone, city, shipping their problems to us. Right now I'm speaking with the city maintenance people about re-bolting the toilets in the restrooms to the floor. We have junkies and needles all over the place. The police officers makes bathroom checks to make sure these people are not hiding in there shooting up, so they look under the stall for feet, consequently the junkies squat on the seats and this has unanchored the commodes from the floor.

"Oh, I am so glad I went into debt and spent four years becoming a master of library science so that I might charge late fees for DVDs and maintain a heroin shooting gallery and homeless latrine! Still, I keep reminding myself, it could be worse—I could be back in Baltimore!"

# Dinduography 101
## The Mapping of Greater Absurdistan

© 2016 James LaFond

Here in the corpse of a capitalist polity now most accurately known as Absurdistan, where the great lie is so bald-faced that our ruler speaks to us of paleface on Dindu aggression even as Dindus slaughter all, it is good to have your bearings.

Absurdistan is broken into three regions:

Dindustan is any municipality or neighborhood with significant level of Dindu infestation in the following toxicity ranges:

Latent infestation:1-3%

Communicable infestation: 4-7%

Contagious infestations: 8-15%

Toxic infestation: 16-25%

Noxious infestation: 25-54%

Terminal infestation: 55-75%

Rampant infestation: 75-90%

Postmortem infestation: 91-97%

Yotopia, sometimes known as Dundidistan, is any area—such as the Northwest Community Action neighborhood in Baltimore—where Dindu population levels are at 98-100%

Whitebreadistan is any area with a less than 1% infestation of state-sponsored, sacred-race criminals.


**Notable regions of Dindustan are not fixed but emerging:**

East Dindustan: the D.C., Baltimore, Camden, Philadelphia corridor

Northeast Dindustan: Jersey-New York-New England

Middle Dindustan: The various shithole cities of Ohio, Indiana and Illinois

North Dindustan: Detroit, Flint and other frozen human latrines of the Great Lakes

South Dindustan: The entire slave master homeland from the Carolinas to Texas

West Dindustan: the Left Coast, where the Dindus are celebrity martyrs

## 'All Da Dindu Day'
### Circadian Hip Hop: The Dinduological Clock

© 2016 James LaFond

What time of day do Dindus attack?

When are they most easily arrested?

First, be warned that there are various anomalies. For instance, at 8:30 this morning—essentially the middle of the Dindu night—I saw a fully dressed for autumn Dindu boy of 7 or 9 years, listlessly sitting by himself in the sweltering July heat at a public park, obviously waiting for the giantess that bred and discarded him to finish pleasing her latest paramour.

### The Dindu Day

11:00 Rise Time

12:00 Pop Tart Time

1:00-3:00 Get Me Mine Time, when weed is bought, smoked, rolled or sold

3-6:00 Cracking Cracker Time, when Dindu mobs play the knockout game, targeting elderly and youth

6-9:00 Foty Time, the favorite hour for getting the second buzz of the day

9-12:00 Polar Bear Time, adult crackers are hunted as the second police shift winds down and officers are loath to make arrests which could keep them tied up after the end of the shift at Central Booking facilities.

12-2:00 Clubbin' Time, when night spots are frequented and a third buzz is submerged in good a drunk

2-5:00 After Hours Time, when illegal basement bars open for business and vacant lots host dice games, rat fishing and gang rapes

5-6:00 Zombie Time, when werewolves and dope fiends wander about and attack anybody and cops and federal officers pick up prostitutes and have sex in parking lots and driveways.

6-8:00 Bedtime, when cops usually kick in your door.

9:00 Court Time, which really messes with your sleep, so you might want to move in with your sister's, mother's, baby's daddy's son for a while...

Keep it real, brutha, and don't eat that paint when it begins to peal.

-A public Service by Doctor Webone Shoop, Board Certified Dinduologist and Registered Dindugraphics Engineer,

https://www.nigms.nih.gov/Education/Pages/Factsh eet_CircadianRhythms.aspx

## Making a Dindudonation
### The Deterrence Officer is Back on Duty in Hamilton after Brazen Daylight Attack

© 2016 James LaFond

The Nigerian priest, who told his parishiners to stop bringing their purses to church to reduce the number of them who would be beaten up and knocked over by Dindu hordlings, gets the douchebag of the month award.

I went down to the ghetto grocery at 1:15 today and noticed that Hamilton was deserted.

Clementine's upscale eatery is now out of business after a six year run.

A deterrence officer, a large, athletic, lone black cop with one of the new replacement cruisers painted in black, was standing with arms crossed outside his car, scanning for Dindus as his car idled with lights on.

More flags have gone up from storefronts and houses, as if people are signaling for help.

I asked Benjamin the hacker, who gets a good three-way vantage from his folding chair on Hamilton, what has happened to cut back pedestrian and motorist traffic even more than the current norm, which is half of the foot and motorized daylight traffic than was normal before the Race Purge of April 2015.

"You know, them young hoppers been crowdin' the corners, staking out on both bus stops, no poleese in sight until after this shit. Yesterday I sittin' here and see this lady down in the gutter, young hoppers dancing around her like fiends at jubilee: punching, stomping—could not tell if she were a black woman or a white, just seen the dress and the heels. She was a church secretary from Saint Dominics—the church where all the ladies been getting' bum-rushed after service—priest led her take the collection box to the BB&T bank right there and they hit her right in front of the door. That stupid priest let the woman out the door with three thousand dollars! Is he stupid?

"I called the poleese, pizza lady call the poleese—but it's over a hundred yards off and I'm old, hiding from them young hoppers my own self. The sad thing was, the people driving through the intersection went around, showed respect for the damned shit act like it were a funeral procession. People where driving their car around the boys dancing on her head, not a young man to step out and crack them niggas on her behalf. Not a *man* in sight. Well the poleese here now. I suppose them hoppers are hunting elsewhere today. We now walk every [white*] lady to her car—even if we not giving her a lift."

"Benjamin calls black women "women" as a general rule, and white women "ladies," unless they are junkies or whores.

Benjamin is from South Carolina, came up in the 1960s, and is thinking of returning. He had cobbled his account together from what little he glimpsed and then what people from the pizza parlor had told him. So I will try and verify it.

As I walked home with my groceries I saw a Dindu scout sitting at the bus stop after the bus pulled up and left. He had his eyes on the cop and seemed to be all of 12, just observing the cop and the foot traffic. I have to hand it to these kids—they are striking late in the morning and early in the afternoon, as if they roll out of their Dindu bunks and go on a raid before

217

breakfast. I suppose I should not be surprised. Their latest offensive does have the full support of their president. This kid struck me as a good little soldier and the beefcake cop had not a clue in the world.

The library up the street has had the windows replaced, and reinforced with wooden bumpers to keep the kids from kicking them in.

# Dindu Down!
## Well Known Harm City Shooter Takes on Cops with Tactical Firearm

© 2016 James LaFond

Dayten Ernest Harper was shooting at someone behind an apartment complex off of Winchester Street in West Baltimore and some nosey cops just couldn't leave well enough alone but had to go get up in his business!

This was just after the Dindu-in-Chief gave his speech about evil white poleese killing innocent Dindus at about 9:30 p,m., Friday night.

The Baltimore police had gotten a tip from the FBI claiming that a credible source informed them that the Black Guerilla Family was discussing ambush options against white Baltimore police. The BPD has not taken this threat seriously and they may be right, as the last time the BGF made such a threat they just used it to bunch up cops in concentrated areas so that they could truck in trailer loads of dope, driving heroin prices down in Baltimore for almost a year.

According to a Vietnam vet who saw this encounter while making coffee in his apartment, the cops gave Dayten a chance to drop his weapon and he shot it out with them instead.

Dayten is the ninth Dindu to get done did by BPD Dindu clearance cyborgs this year. The two cybernetic organisms who put him down have been temporarily unplugged and sent back to base for a psychological refit. Hopefully they will be refinished in urban ebony camo-paint.

Thanks to the BGF threat and the nationwide black-on-blue insurgency, BPD cops are now rolling two deep, which means police coverage is halved for all calls and observable intelligence is also cut in half, which means the regular citizens are in heightened peril as the cops protect themselves as an understandable first priority. Dindus have been looking for cop free openings to begin mob attacks on white civilians, and have been successful in increasing their "get me some" to "got my ass caught" ratio, thus far.

The BPD chopper has been over my house for a half hour as cop cars cruise in a grid centered one block to my south.

Thank you WellRead Ed, for this heads up.

Police Shootings

http://www.baltimoresun.com/news/maryland/crime/bs-md-ci-police-shooting-folo-20160715-story.html

## Dindu Warrior MREs
### The Food Urban Martyrs Are Made Of

© 2016 James LaFond

Just like any combat athlete, the Dindu warrior goes into battle with his opponent, the body-armored "poleese," with a body rigorously conditioned through training, like banking old ladies at Saint Dominic's church, and stealing your brutha's baby's fatha's weed while he's laid up with Mamma.

But a warrior is more than his training. He literaly is what he consumes. So here you go, Yo, if yo want to sign up for White Daddy Soros' Black Lives Matter Brigade, "fuel the fuck up" on the top ten Dindu field rations:

#10: Steel reserve malt liquor

#9: Newport menthol filter kings

#8: Blunt of weed, made with Dutch Masters flavored cigars

#7: Fruit flavored soda pop, Sunny Delight orange-flavored drink or grape Kool Aid

#6: Pop Tarts

#5: Snack Cakes—Little Debbie's Sweet white ass being the preferred brand

#4: Butterfinger or Snickers candy bars

#3: Honey Nut Cheerios

#2: Steamed skrimps

#1: Ramen Noodles

This is Webone Shoop, your source for militant outfitting advice for the coming Dark Age—en I mean that shit literal.

# The Yo-Hell Lease Prize
**Cyril is the World's First Recipient of the Yo-Hell Lease Prize to be Bestowed by the National Dinduological Association**

© 2016 James LaFond

Cyril has been awarded this august honor based on the following linguistic formula:

Cyril July 18, 2016 7:56 AM EDT

"Go to Google Translate.

"Select English as the first language, Welsh as the second.

Enter "black man."

"Enjoy."

Cyril, you may come to Harm City, in East Dindustan, to collect your prize at any time. You will be escorted by Webone Shoop on a "liquor store jaunt" during which you may sample a forty of malt liquor on the sidewalk in front of each stop. If the Poleese attempt to enforce the open-container law, Weboon will then coach you on how to argue with them in such a way as to maximize your chance for a successful "poleese ruthality" law suit.

# The Home Invasion Equation
### 4yrs in jail, damages: Finnish man sentenced after defending against home invasion: An Anarcho-Tyranny Case Study

© 2016 James LaFond

The single most shocking trend in studying violence in the Baltimore Metropolitan Area is that, over the past five years, all three police departments I monitor, and the reporting media, have blatantly reclassified and misreported home invasions—which are the most heinous crime as rape, murder, abduction and torture fall under the home invasion heading with regularity—as assaults, robberies, burglaries and simple destruction of property. There can be no greater evidence that your government wants you to live in terror than this simple bookkeeping set of immoral gymnastics.

Below is a recent and most ridiculous example of this State practice from Finland. The man in question was defending his wife against three aggressive criminals armed with a gun and bats. He used a knife, did not kill any of the intruders, and has been stuck with a prison term and a fine much greater than theirs. Note that all four parties were regarded as committing a crime, and they did engage in criminal activity, for in a civilized society, only the authorized proxy aggressor—that is the police/military—may use force, period. Every time you defend yourself in the U.S. or abroad, in other communist nations, you are committing a crime. The only question is will the Court make an exception in your case and excuse your crime as justifiable?

Anarcho-Tyranny is nothing more than the full flowering of that monstrous beast, Civilization, which we so idiotically worship.

In some posts over the past year I have written some things that some readers have taken as crass bragging or as an expression of a fatalistic death wish, in regards to fighting the police. I have done neither. What I have done is simply state that I will not be that guy that get's imprisoned or jailed for defending himself. I have drastically curtailed my daily activities so as to avoid having to defend myself against Dindus and put up with the ever-present police harassment leveled at poor urban palefaces, the combination of which is maddening. Mentally, my back is already to the wall and I'm too damned old and fat to outrun prime buck, or even over-weaned whelp, Dindus. Seriously, if I defend against such a home invasion and a responding cop tells me I have the right to remain silent, he will have just predicted what the near future holds for both of us—eternal silence. My reason for stating such a thing is, in case I fail to prevent such a situation from overtaking me, that my Sons will not think I just went insane and committed suicide by cop, but that I was abiding by a principal of personal autonomy.

https://www.rt.com/news/352236-jail-finland-court-robbery/#

# Little Debbie's Big Idea
## Dealing with Little Dindu Bitches or Dindettes

© 2016 James LaFond

I stopped at the Ghetto Mart for coconut water today and saw a sight.

Little Debbie is a big chick of Swedish descent who works as a cashier at a ghetto supermarket in Harm City, Maryland. She noticed that the lady who she had just checked out—a small, Dindu bitch in cut off jeans, wife beater and flip-flops with her hair woven with fake braids—had a box of fried chicken hidden under her shopping cart. She pointed to the security guard, who stopped the woman and asked her to pay for the chicken.

The little, 18-year-old-looking Dindette then began screaming, and swearing at Debbie, told her she wanted a refund, that it was Debbie's fault for not seeing the chicken, and that she was "from Wess Balmore, bitch," en we can take dis shit outside, where I'll whoop yo white ass—bitch!"

Debbie stepped out from behind the register and said, "Let's go, Bitch. I'll grab that wiglett of yours and scrub the sidewalk with your face!"

The Dindette, looking up at the husky paleface broad, then seemed to think better of her challenge, set the box of unpaid chicken on the register back, and left, looking over her shoulder nervously.

I love shopping at the Ghetto Mart.

# Nadia's Baby in Blue
### Rise of the Dindu God

© 2016 James LaFond

Nadia works in an office in downtown Baltimore for a private employer. Her best friend's brother is a Baltimore City Police officer. With her friend worried every night that her brother will end up targeted by a Dindu ambush, Nadia wished to show some support, so dressed up her infant girl in a police patrolman's hat—the toy kind for kids, gotten at the dollar store—and posted her picture on FaceBook.

An upper-middleclass, black coworker happened upon Nadia's FaceBook post and became greatly offended at the cute paleface infant in blue and logged a complaint with management, who informed Nadia that she was not permitted to make racist of politically volatile posts if she wished to maintain her employment!

The world is truly upside down.

I still hate cops.

Earlier this month a big Dindu called the BPD on me for the crime of standing up to his big ass when he walked up behind me and felt better of whatever he had had in mind and diverted his course away from me. Within five minutes I had a blonde, cunt, whore BPD cop screaming at me with her hand on her gun for the crime of being a man waiting for the bus in a Dindu Ethical Preserve.

Dindus are my lifelong enemies.

Cops are my lifelong enemies.

I wish them both success in their struggle, but hold out little hope that either side will gain the upper hand. Instead, they will fumble at each other until the fools of this nation finally take one side or the other and demand a federal police force. By then, if I'm still around I'll be getting attacked by Dindus while I hobble along on my cane and then get tazed by federal pigs for the crime of caning the sacred martyr race of our degenerate age.

America, the latest nation to degenerate in the great cycle of sick societies, get it over with—join your children in the worship the of the Dindu God, squatting on his phallic throne, a parody of Man battling the modern parody of the lawman.

# False Calls
## Dindu Psychological Operations

© 2016 James LaFond

In the past week I have read two local news stories
and have gathered three local accounts that confirm a
trend I first notice earlier this month [July, 2016].
Dindu psychological operations specialists have bee
calling Baltimore Area 911 lines and calling the cops
on people, mostly on black people, claiming they have
guns, bats or knives and that they are attacking
people.

The first time I experienced such a thing was when
Chuck, Dominick and myself were sparring at
Patapsco Senior High School, on a Sunday morning,
on the shot put area of the track. Two EMT douche
bags pulled over and began harassing us, telling us
what we were doing was unsafe and against the law

and that we were pussies. We ignored them. Ten minutes later four pigs pulled up and walked out to question us. I could imagine what this scene would be like today. We'd be getting executed on our knees. The one athletic cop who was not a pussy, asked many intelligent questions and we had a nice conversation. Then my wife, who was there observing, suggested the cop try sparring with me and I almost shit.

Yes, this is a type of harassment in which manginas and other such douche bags use the robotic police to harass men they cannot deal with ona physical level. But what the Dindus is doing is brilliant.

1. Kill cops.

2. Have criminal organizations threaten to kill more cops.

3. Watch the cops bunch up so that you can attack more uncovered taregts.

4. Now call the cops and sick them on a non-criminal, diverting at least two cops and hopefully getting an innocent person shot so that they may serve as martyr food for thc propaganda machine.

# Dawn in Dindustan

At this point the Dindu game is so much more sophisticated than the Pig game, one is tempted to surmise that federal operatives are advising the Dindu cadres. It is a fact that the DOJ announced their investigation of the BPD a day before local gangs threatened to kill cops, which bunched them up and enabled the Race Purge which was never reported upon and already forgotten by the few that no of it, even though it remains ongoing. The DOJ also advised the mayor to stand her cops down, which ruined their morale. I will finish Dawn in Dindustan with a litany of recent Dindu strikes on palefaces and black men.

But first we must delve into Dinduosophy.

The Wicked Witch of the Left wishes to be Queen of the Hive and requires Dindu war drones to pave her way. Yo, be a joiner and get whitey!

-Webone Shoop reporting from Harm City, Maryland

# Dinduosophy
## The Theoretical Basis for the Dindu

© 2016 James LaFond

Dinduosophy is merely the study of the beliefs that Dindus hold that other peoples typically do not share. The International Association of Dinduosophy has rated each of these beliefs as untrue, true, or partially true.

1. Jews were black until they interbred with the white devils. Untrue

2. Jesus, was therefore black. Untrue

3. All peoples native to Africa are black—there being no Berbers, Cappoids, Arabs or Malaysians. Untrue

[Granted that most American whites are just as stupid as Dindus and believe this to be truc also.]

4. Hanno was black, when in fact he was of Phoenician descent. Untrue

5. That the CIA targeted black communities in American Inner cities for crack addiction. True

6. That Nazi Scientists working for the U.S. government invented HIV to kill blacks. Untrue

7. That police are not trained, equipped, organized and managed to protect and serve anybody, but rather to wage a domestic war against drug addicts and drug suppliers. True

8. The police are more likely to attack black suspects than whites. Untrue.

[Look, Tyrone 4 times as many pale faces are killed by pigs every year than are blacks. In my own neighborhood, over the past five years, I have seen three arrests of blacks, and four arrests of whites. The cops began by speaking with the black guys, and then got physical after the idiots argued. With the white guys, they just physically grabbed them without saying much—just bam, getting stuffed into the back of a car with no due process.]

9. That white people hate black people, when in fact most whites worship black culture and imitate their degenerate antics at every opportunity. Untrue

10. That the only thing preventing the wholesale slaughter of Dindukind by 10% of American, paleface male kind, are the very police that Dindus hate and attack. True

[How better to keep that protection against real white boys and rednecks, who are hated by the majority sissy population of whites, then to scare the sissy whites into calling for strengthened police forces as a deterrent against the soft threat that real warriors know is the least martial race on planet earth, the only people to fail to fight their way out of their homeland for all of the ages of Man?]

11. That only black people have been enslaved in modern times, which the vast majority of paleface fools also believe, despite the fact that 2 million Russian girls are getting ass-raped in the Middle East this weekend.

As you can see, Dindus get most of the small points and historical trivia dead wrong, but are far superior to palefaces when it comes to seeing clearly the power structure currently in flux.

Long live Dindustan!

Long live the Dinduman!

# The Gray Ghost Never Rests

**Three Officers Cleared of Charges Related to Freddie Gray's Martyrdom Face Internal Affairs Probe**

© 2016 James LaFond

Montgomery County police will head the investigation.

The slain martyr of the rising Black Lives Matter Cult, and one day to be the pained image hanging on the walls of the sanctuaries of a world religion, Freddie Gray, is still reaching into the perfidious present from beyond the Hip Hop grave to avenge himself upon the Baltimore City Pigs who did him good and wrong.

Although two vanilla wafers and their chocolate filling have been dropped from the Bitch Queen State's Attorney's prosecutor bag of tricks, as the judge throws these poorly made and corruptly constructed cases out the legal window, the Mulattress mayor has assured her criminal constituents—including the thugs who had her nephew murdered because she wouldn't play ball a few years back—that the maximum internal weight of the BPD will be brought to bear on the evil men who gave Freddie vinegar to drink when he gasped for water.

This will probably just make the Dindu base in Baltimore more angry at the all black establishment that somehow represents Whitey, because it is very doubtful that fellow cops are going to elect to bar these cops from returning to duty.

Also, concurrently, five of the six charged cops [one of the chocolate cops had a mistrial] are suing the State's Attorney!

# Dindutopia
## What Would an All Black Regional America Look Like?

© 2016 James LaFond

"Hey James looks like this an opportunity for you to do some serious speculative ethnography. Much in the same vein as Sir Thomas Moore's 'Utopia'. Like what would Omowale's 'Blacktopia' look like? What system of government would it be likely to have? What would be the major political divisions? What would its economy be based on. What would its major exports be? Further, since we already know that even black people don't want to live in majority black neighborhoods (or countries), how would this new nation prevent 'black flight'?"

-Jeremy Bentham

January, 1, 2025, the fences of Dindutopia—around the former states of Alabama, Mississippi, Louisiana and Tennessee, with the Mississippi and Ohio Rivers and the Gulf Coast greatly aiding the control of egress and ingress necessary for a tariff-based society to flourish—go up.

There are no taxes in Dindutopia—none, beat that Whitey!

There are no police in Dindutopia—free at last, free at last, Lord, free at last!

There is no capital of Dindutopia as it is a peripheral nation.

Dindutopia has no extradition treaty with The White States of America.

There are no prisons or jails, drug laws, liquor laws, traffic laws—it is a free country. Can you say that, Whitey?

No, your taxpaying ass cannot.

There is a government of Dindutopia that occupies the half-mile wide government zone that circles the nation, fenced on the inside, which means that the main perk you get for joining the government—which is done by buying shares and investing in the government—is waterfront access and the ability to travel freely into the White States of America to buy stuff that the residents of Dindutpia cannot produce.

Aside from buying into the government, the State itself is financed according to the following scheme:

1. White people—no matter what they have done—can get into Dindutopia for 50K

2. Black people may enter Dindutopia for free!

3. Asians get in for 10k each

4. Latinos get in for 25k

5. Africans are not allowed the fuck in, alright!

6. Whites may leave for a million.

7. Blacks may apply to leave. Their application will then be sent to White America. If White America wants them, they have to pay the Dindutopian government 1 million to get their Negro back. If White America does not want their black ass they only have to pay Dindutopia 10k a year to keep that Dindu in Dindutopia.

8. Asians may leave for 100k

9. Latinos may leave for 50k

Every black person that moves into Dindutopia gets free housing and access to whatever they want to take from anyone else, including cars, food, money, sex...

Every black woman may apply for welfare, which pays 2k per month, cash, bitch.

**That's Dindutopia, you have read all you need to know, next immigrant, please**

The free housing is that Filipino Marine surplus pup-tent that the big brother handed you before he chained the gate behind you. Welfare is paid to all females their first month [See Snoop Dog at The Big-Ass Easy. He pays all his girls 2k their first month—en don't you be showin' up all fat en sloppy ether.] For additional welfare you must see the welfare agency— as soon as we hire her. If you would like to apply to be the welfare agency, fill out your qualifications on the back of this survey, place it in your empty Pepsi bottle, and toss it in the river. Our Human resources agency in New Orleans will process your application. If you would like to be the Human Resources Director state that on your application.

Thank you for moving to Dindutopia—now move the fuck out da way!

## Dintutopia Addendum
### Or What was Implied and Therefore Not Obvious Enough for Your White Ass to Comprehend

© 2016 James LaFond

As a peripheral, tariff based entity, the Government of Dindutopia does not intrude upon the sanctity of Hip Hop life, which is, after all, the ruling ethos of Dindutopia, which explains the exports, which are not subject to tariff by the White States of America and other racist polities. Have a few clues below:

1. Taxation is an individual expression of ho-macking dominance. You may "tax dat ass" or not, yo. You may pay that tax, bitch, or pay some bigga nigga to tax his ass!

2. Exports are limited to what Dindutopians produce: weed, blunts, meth—if we can get some smart white

boys up in here to cook that shit up—rap, hip hop, R&B, Tyler Perry movies, and deals.

3. It is known that White America will make a huge investment in Dindutopia by supporting the drug trade and by building manufacturing centers free of all regulations and other government bullshit. Since Dindutopians do not work, that means these companies will have to pay the Dindutopian Government for each Hispanic and Asian it ships in to do the work.

So there, back at ya, cracka.

# Rise Up or Run
**Street Christ & Olympic Hopeful Oppressed by Latina-Cracka Conspiracy: A Clarion Call to Rise Against The Man by Webone Shoop**

© 2016 James LaFond

This morning at 4:45, deep in the hood, at the scene of last year's mighty victory over the faceless functionaries of The Man, one of the many reincarnations of Black Jesus among the crackers—I don't want to hear about Jesus not being a Hindu. He's Jesus, and since he's black, can do what the hell he wants!—walked up to cold-hearted Butch, the frozen food man, who was taking his break out front, and asked him for a dollar. Butch, busy counting out his ones, told Black Jesus, coldly, "Don't have any dollars, sorry."

The down-trodden street Christ, suffering under the Whiteman's sins, then stepped over to the unnamed Mexican chick, who cleans the floors, as she took advantage of Butch's angry shadow to step outside for some fresh air, and asked, "You gotta dolla, miss?"

The little Latina, already swayed by the money of The Man and hateful of a brutha in need, then looked up to him and said, "No dolla."

To which he spat, "Fuckin' bitch!"

Driven once again to shame himself by the evil hand of White Devil Daddy on the back of his innocent neck, the street Christ staggered off in shame, still unable to convince a single devil soul, white or brown, to redeem themselves before the Lord.

A short time later, a young athlete, Rejuvean by name, entered the White Devil nest, where black women were enslaved, chained to the registers and counters by the invisible bonds of the Whiteman's cruel desire. In the name of the New Afrikan Resistance, Rejuvean showed how tragic the tyranny of white oppression is. Instead of playing ball at a private high school, like all of them privileged white-boys, Rejuvean is reduced to demonstrating his quarterbacking qualifications in such forlorn hope attacks against The Man's infrastructure.

Rejuvean headed right to the health and beauty aisle, so that he could resell Dove bar soap and hair straightener on the street and hopefully raise enough money to move his mother, who is sick with cancer, to a nice island in the Pacific where no white people will mess with her. Unfortunately, as he loaded up his hat and spare shirt with bars of soap and bundled them together—there was that mean looking white dude stocking the frozen food case and grilling him like he was doing something wrong, when in fact, even after this reparations recovery strike, America would still owe him like $40,000, with interest compounded daily for like four hundred years, so he wasn't even wrong.

Being a realist, Rejuvean knew he would not be able to get back out the front door. He walked into the stockroom, located the employee lockers, found that his brother must have accidentally left a pair of bolt-cutters in the side pocket of his cargo shorts, and was struck with an inspiration. He snapped the lock on an employee locker belonging to some bitch-ass-nigga named Dante and put his work shirt on. Unfortunately, as Rejuvean pulled on the shirt and some white voice came over the intercom talking some shit about "Baltimore City Police to the stockroom," he discovered that Dante was a giant, bitch-ass-nigga, because that shirt came down about his knees. He saw daylight though, just around the corner past that wire rack that—oh no, yo—was getting caught up on that giant bitch-ass-nigga work shirt. He managed to get himself free as some smirking white employee man stood between him and the door with his arms crossed.

Free, free at fucking last, Rejuvean cradled his reparations package like Ray Rice before the White NFL leadership screwed him out of a spot on the team, and ran right at this old cracker, knowing that he was going to fake his old ass out and—blam, smash, crash... Yes, indeed, this is unfortunately how so many Reparations Recovery Agents are thwarted in pursuit of their righteous goal, by some big-ass traitor-nigga in a police uniform blindsiding their ass and kneeling on their head while slapping on The Man's shackles.

What more can I say than to point out to you non-militant bruthas, that if Rejuvean had been but one of three strike team members, his sacrifice would not have been in vain, because as big as this traitor was, he wasn't tackling three dudes at the same time.

-Webone Shoop, edumacating your ass

# Dinduroics
## Alley Atbar and the Four Thieves and Seven Other Stories of Dindu Heroes

© 2016 James LaFond

The following tales all happened in the early summer of 2016 in Eastern Baltimore County, where Reparations Recovery Measures are being driven hard by young warriors, unfortunately resulting in some collateral damage. The roll call of heroes is below.

Jerold and Lamonte were playing ball on the court on South Marlyn, when they got in a heated argument. Jerold can't fight worth shit, so while Lamonte was whooping his ass, he stabbed him in the hip and ran off. True to The Cause, when the police rolled up and questioned Lamonte, he did not have any idea who the stabber was and had never seen him before.

Some sorry-ass white dude got off the last #23 bus out of the City at 1:30 a.m. Sunday and walked down

Middleborough Road, like this shit was still acceptable. Having recently solidified their territory, the M-3 set dispatched their four youngest runners to bring this dude down, which was easily accomplished as the dumbass tried to push them away and cover his head at the same time. In about 10 seconds the cracker was laying and praying on the ground as he was relieved of his backpack, phone, wallet, money and all of his clothes except for his underpants. One of the warriors was later arrested by police and was leaving the court house with his mother by noon on Monday.

Later that same Sunday, at 1:30 in the afternoon, a cracker was walking down Middleborough Road when a three-man strike team rolled up in a car. Two of the young soldiers jumped out and went right for him, asserting their territorial dominance. When the redneck on foot decided to throw hands the brothers punished him. The smaller dude drew his knife [every strike team should have a knife man] cut the dude's arm, and then made a tactical retreat to their combat vehicle, the driver of which sped off.

At 1:30 on Saturday morning, out at Ambo Circle, some dude of unknown race was smoking outside his place, when a dude he knew and two other dudes approached him. The dude he knew distracted him and the other two attacked, beating him down and taking the money he expected would have bought his high for the night. If you move out to the suburbs to hunt crackers this is a good way to set them up for beat downs, by using bait-friends. If you have moved out to the suburbs to hunt crackers, don't get in the habit of stepping outside to speak to people at night, especially if there are dudes you don't know accompanying him. A lot of dudes forget why they are moving into a white area and start to attack each other. For this reason I suggest you buy your weed from white dudes.

At 9:30 on a weekday night a white dude was walking out Eastern Boulevard toward the 7-11 when two brothers rode up to him on bikes and punched him out without even dismounting, even leaning down off the bikes to clean out his pockets and get his money. This dude was so low class he didn't even have a cell phone and deserved what he got for not being able to fight. The boys then rode off, completing this very Comanche-like raid in fine style.

At 3:40 p.m. on Saturday afternoon, as hundreds of cars full of scared white people and don't give a shit right people, drove by, a can't fight white boy was walking along with his face in his smart phone when a big, black, righteous brother, rising up from 400 years of white oppression like a titan of retribution, just slammed his fist into that brittle cracker face and took his shit! Unfortunately, the police were called by someone and our hero was arrested soon thereafter.

At 5 in the morning on a Wednesday, a white boy and his sweetheart were taking a walk. Unbeknownst to their can't fight asses, a heroic sufferer of systemic white racism had decided to strike back at his oppressors and had hidden in the bushes at the corner of the apartment building. When they turned the corner he rose up behind them and cut them both with his knife, before beating a tactical retreat. This brother got away free to strike another day.

Alley Atbar was walking along after getting off work down at the mall where he works for evil Whitey. Alley is a mixed race dude. He further demonstrated his loyalty to the evil white parent by not packing up with homeboys and casting a menacing shadow, but by walking along minding his own business and expecting no trouble, as if he was a full-blooded white boy back in Leave it to Beaver Land. Guilty of the crime of not behaving like a hip hop hero, Alley Atbar was targeted for redistribution, having been adjudged white by the pilot of the strike vehicle, which was occupied by a full four-man team of Reparations Recovery Agents. As Alley turned the corner onto Silver Spring from Perry Hall Boulevard, he found himself in the midst of a swarm of rabid hoodrats. Just as the black in him started to rise to the top and he began to fight, the little bastards ran away with his backpack.

There you have it, son, know what team you are on and comport yourself accordingly.

-Webone Shoop advisoring on behalf of your black ass

# Going to School in Harm City
**Doris Recounts Her First Day in a Desegregated Baltimore City High School, Circa 1978**

© 2016 James LaFond

My older sister didn't go to school with blacks, so there was no one to tell me what it would be like. In my first period, on the first day, in homeroom class, this tall black kid sat next to me. I was uncomfortable, having a hard time concentrating on the teacher, because I could tell—out of the corner of my eye—that he was staring at me, not even looking at the teacher.

I put my hand up next to me eye and just looked straight ahead, trying to pay attention to the teacher.

After a while he pulled my hand down [he was seated to her left], which got me angry. When I turned to look at him he had this long, stupid grin on his face, his pants were down around his knees under his desk [open, one piece desk-chairs] and he was masturbating, going at it—had even brought lubricant to school with him—while he was staring at me and grinning. He kept doing it, finished it even and the class went on! It was like being in a mad house. [Puts hands over ears as she shakes her head]

That was the start of four years of terror. These big, ugly, smelly, black boys were always trying to have sex with you, the black girls made it impossible to use the bathroom, because they'd rip your hair out or your head and the teachers just pretended nothing was happening.

I'm never setting foot back in Baltimore.

*This interview was recorded in 1996, one of 19 remaining in my original unpublished notes for The Violence Project.*

# 'How Were These Numbers Obtained?'

## A Man Question from Anthony on James' Numbers on Racial Violence in Baltimore

© 2016 James LaFond

Anthony commented on 'I'm Confused about Race and Violence' Sep-30-2016 3:09 PM UTC

### *'I'm Confused About Race And Violence'*

### James Answers

As stated in the article, this information is all obtained by my own experience or from people I interview or casually speak to. This is an admittedly haphazard process, but is at least honest and more importantly, puts violence in actual perspective, instead of using the bogus FBI protocol of acts per 100,000 people. For instance, it is far more important that you are white and outside on foot at night in a black area than that 200 out of 100,000 people in your area reported being robbed at gunpoint last year and that these reports were not down graded to simple assault, lost altogether, or, in the case of a successful defense, listed as a mutual combat and thrown out.

These numbers are only from first person and eye-witness reports, as the identity of attackers and victims is obscured in press coverage and the police stats are intentionally juked, therefore I cannot use news reports for sources.

These numbers are skewed toward a white readership, as, unlike my original survey, I now have access to less black victims than white victims, as I no longer work on a black crew and the young blacks I take the bus with and who work in other departments at my job, refuse to speak with me, because I terrify them. Since I do not demonstrate fear of blacks, most blacks regard me as a maniacal Nazi. The Baltimore racial divide is continuing to expand, making it harder and harder for me to befriend blacks with each passing week.

These numbers are small.

I should have at least 500, but wrote this as soon as I hit 100, so as not to stress my math-averse brain.

These numbers do not meet any of the criteria for deriving statistics that could hold up under peer review. But I'm just a high school dropout without peers, so that does not concern me.

However, according to FBI Supervisory Agent Tom Petrowski, who interviewed me about my methodology in 2001, all law enforcement numbers except for murders are filtered in various ways, including cops not having the time to do all of the paperwork on the violence that they are personally involved in. In my original study of 1675 acts of violence conducted from June 1996 through May 2000—for which I used a 48 point checklist and discarded any encounter I could not verify 8 facts about—I did not even look at race unless it involved, knife use, gun use and mob attacks.

My most recent work with numbers—all of which one could find fault with, as I am not a statistician and I do not have the logistical means to do a broad-based survey, but use the very crude method of recording all violence experienced and witnessed by myself and those I come into contact with—can be found in

40,000 Years from Home. My entire, extensive, personal violence history is included in that book and occupies over 5 chapters.

## 40,000 Years from Home

https://www.amazon.com/ooo-Years-Home-James-LaFond-ebook/dp/B01KCVLGZY/ref=sr_1_34?s=books&ie=UTF8&qid=1475340336&sr=1-34&keywords=james+lafond

I'm just sampling here, but, I'm conducting the only sampling that I know of for working class mixed-race aggression in an urban setting that is not biased by law enforcement manipulation, YouTube video selection or academic stipulation, but is rather biased according to circumstance.

Furthermore, these numbers are now badly out of date and represent a transitory trend in violence that included the Baltimore Purge and Riots of 2015. The Purge is still ongoing and represents a paradigm shift in aggression dynamics in Baltimore, but the riots are done. So, I should do another study, but would rather just focus on individual stories and survival advice. I am hoping that Baltimore, since it is the 25th largest city with the 8th largest police force and is ahead on the violence curve—indeed, we finished first in murders last year—will serve as an example of what may come of other similar cities under similar pressures.

How did this process begin?

Read When You're Food, available in print in two editions and from our online store for only $5.

# Dindu You
## Aggression at the Register in Dindustan

© 2016 James LaFond

*The following is forwarded from a neighborhood website.*

McDonald's 1619 Joppa rd

from Ridgeleigh • 2d ago

Please pay close attention next time you go there. We pulled money out of the ATM and went there for food. The girl at the window took my money then the manager came back and told me it was fake. "The money pen left a big black mark on it," is what the manager said. This is true. Yellow if good and black like a sharpie if it is bad. Having a background in retail and use the money pen often, I asked to see it. He said he didn't have time for that. So my wife asked him again. He said its company policy not to give it back or show it, so I started out the door to call the police and he brings the $20 and gives it to my wife. And what do you know. No black mark. No yellow. No nothing. He stapled a paper to it with counterfeit written on it. He was trying to steal my money!! Just wonder how many people he had who don't do this too, and let him get away with it.

# 'He's Scared'
## Paleface Priestess Worships Dindu God

**Northeast Baltimore, 10/15/2016**

Today a fine young black man, named Oliver, took time off of work to open the boxing gym up for Sean, who had driven down from PA—to train. I asked him how his contracting business was doing and he said, "I just hired my first guy."

I responded, "Have you fired him yet?"

He answered, "No, not until this afternoon," shaking his head, recalling my warning that he would have a long road to hoe putting a crew together from among young men.

Today I helped a fine young black man, named Isaac, learn how to stick fight, gave him advice, a fencing mask and agreed to help him with his boxing.

Erique, a fine young black man, who I also coach, expressed worry about my health, my situation, asked me to call him if I needed anything...

I'm not exactly the atypical, privileged, white oppressor of black youth.

## South Baltimore, late 1990s, Hanover Street and Fort Avenue

Once, when two negroes tried to stop me and make them show them what was in my pockets, and I did, and it turned out not to be a knot roll of money but a big fucking knife, it scared these younger, larger men. As they moaned about my attack, a white bitch of the rich, gentrified kind came out of her house and called the pigs on me. Off I went running through the alleys, streets, parks and finally hid in the freezer walk-in at the store I worked at while the pigs questioned my coworkers about the presence of the long-haired white-man with a knife...

As a man who walks in areas where it is unsafe to walk on the sidewalk, I understand walking in the street, but not during the day, in a low crime, suburban location. This habit of walking in the street in black ghettos can be—and should be—discarded when in white suburbs, where cars are more dangerous than pedestrians. But the white whore taking this video should be given to the men of Papua New Guinea.

Below are some other videos by Colin documenting The Hunt for Whitey.

https://www.youtube.com/watch?v=dTfZepLVi3M

Banking A Limo Driver

https://www.youtube.com/watch?v=7xaxAc6N_Qg

Murdering a Lonely White Man

https://www.youtube.com/watch?v=n0B1lJDmc-Q

# Harm County Pigskin
## A Holiday Police Linebacker Strategy

© 2016 James LaFond

For 15 months after the Baltimore Riots we have rarely seen police at the supermarket where I work unless they are picking up lunch. They also no longer patrol the foot approaches to the store, one of which, Old Eastern Avenue, has become the crime mob attack corridor in the area. What they are doing, I can only guess, other than policing the primary street of Eastern Boulevard for traffic violations. I do suspect that manpower has been loaned to higher priority Towson precinct, under siege by packs of transplanted Baltimore City criminals.

So, I was fascinated, three nights after Thanksgiving, to arrive to work and see a heavy police presence on the lot.

One cruiser parks in the recess of the L-shaped strip mall, able to observe both foot approaches and all four vehicle entry points. His lights are on.

Just beyond the lot skulk two darkened cop cruisers with lights off, laying in wait.

Inside, I asked a coworker if he had spoken with any of the cops about their being stationed here. He told me that the cops informed him that they were expecting flash [black] mob raids on strip malls, as well as "other trouble," which we took to mean car-mobile armed robbery crews and gun-and knife-armed posing thugs.

Recently, in another county strip mall there was a shooting. When holidays come to Dindustan and Mamma has her "man" over for "scrimps en liquor en weed," she doesn't want her grown-ass hoodrats hanging around, so they loiter all night in and around strip malls and other businesses, usually committing acts of aggression, whether for sport or for profit.

"Welcome to Dindustan, yo. Be cool dough, ova behine da Chineese joint dere be some popo."

## Appendix: Reader Provided Research Links

### 'The White Minstrel'
### THE GLOBAL FAVELA BY GREGORY HOOD •
### JULY 6, 2016

© 2016 James LaFond

'The Most Deeply Insulated Shitlib'

-Gregory Hood

Gregory hood is quick becoming my favorite columnist. The only thing I have to add to this article is that Brazil has one thing that America lacks: testicles. I'll take Hell as a man over Heaven as an eunuch.

Brazil—as Mister Hood points out—is an excellent model for ancient style social stratification in a technology-driven economy, with the poor ripping into each other while the rich fortify, which leaves no place for the middle and working class. A recent survey in my neighborhood in Baltimore Maryland has indicated that one house is barred and "gated" for every house that is abandoned or put up for sale. If you have any stock options on decorative door and window bars, buy in.

http://www.radixjournal.com/journal/2016/7/6/the-global-favela-2

### 'Respect for the Sanctity of Life'
### Dindustan News: Harm City Tax Farmers Seek Maximum Biomass

© 2016 James LaFond

In another philosophical win for atheistic materialism, all life [including the Yellow Fever virus, I suppose] has been declared sacred by the Baltimore City Mayor, who has issued new policing directives targeted at overzealous cops. Admittedly, Baltimore cops have been primarily involved in senselessly beating the shit out of non-violent criminals—guilty, for instance, of being born black or being white in a Dindu annexed area—for the past 50 years. Now, all of a sudden cops are supposed to talk to screaming Dindus as the Dindu horde swells in strength. Also, any cop who sees another using too much force, must now take the side of the target person.

This attitude did save me from a raging bitch cop two weeks ago, as she screamed at me with her hand on her gun for no reason whatsoever, as I peacefully waited for the bus. The big-assed, blonde bitch was then calmed down by a smooth- talking Mandingo cop and I was saved. So, I personally should benefit from this initiative as the crime of being an underdressed, paleface pedestrian in Dindustan is apparently an affront to porcine kind.

In the long term, this initiative is about federalizing policing in urban centers. For the cops will now step back even further from their duty of keeping rampaging criminals in check and focus on policing non-threatening citizens who are unlikely to talk back or resist. This will render regular police into the equivalent of unarmed security guards, unable to stand up to gang sets and mobs. The gang detail will be diverted to federal agencies and the mobs will be taken care of by the military whenever they become a threat to the government or news reporters. There is no way this was a locally hatched policy. The entire time she has been in power, the Mulattress Mayor has been taking her crime fighting directions directly from the DOJ.

This is Jungle Jim reporting from Dindustan.

PS: Oliver Wendell Hayes has informed me that he is setting up a YouTube channel with a Jungle Jim theme, which will feature videos of our ebony and ivory exploration of Harm City and other Dindustan municipalities. Actually, I think I'd be more fitting for the role of Skipper or Tamba, and Kaseem is obviously running the local liquor store, but duty calls...

**Jungle Jim Intro**

https://www.youtube.com/watch?v=ShU-vbwtb3o

**'Granny Merkel is Making Her Move'**
**Plans for a European Dindustate Emerge**

© 2016 James LaFond

"I know you hate the English, but they made the right call."

-Damocles, UK Correspondent for Jungle Jim News

http://www.express.co.uk/news/politics/683739/EU-referendum-German-French-European-superstate-Brexit

Well, in my defense, my hatred of the English is purely recreational! I am a quarter Limey, you know! I have been following this with Molyneux and the Info Wars guy. It seems that the Anglo hostages aren't out of the Empire of Guilt yet. I had no idea that the Irish voted out of the EU twice and got sucked back into the amoral gravity well both times.

Oh, in checking up on Stefan's guest's claim that 8,000 Jews have fled France this year, I found out that France has the third largest population of Jews behind Israel and the U.S. and that those 8,000 went to Israel, and that 25,000 have fled to London.

Now, as far as that Hag Merkel goes, goddess of her own geriatric superstate, if she were black and good looking, this would look like the dream of Yasmeena, Queen of the Yagas in Almuric.

Thanks, Damocles, I'm glad to have a correspondent in the UK.

**Before Skynet Rises**
**Caucasian Extinction Event Missives from**
**Nero the Pict**

© 2016 Nero the Pict

Started watching the "Last Whites of the East End". I had to hit pause and send you these links. If you are not familiar with Enoch Powell's "Rivers of Blood" speech you might want to check this out.

Rivers of blood BBC Doc

https://www.youtube.com/watch?v=9hePwGKMgfM

Surprisingly even handed by BBC standards. There are nods to the PC as is obligatory but overall worth your time

England- Whose England? (Part 1 of 2)

https://www.youtube.com/watch?v=L8M6FEu4_HY

England Whose England Part 2 of 2

https://www.youtube.com/watch?v=R7Sst54gQq8

The last is a two-parter. A couple of newsreels that some anti immigration outfit shot in the early-mid 70's (judging by the hair styles etc.). Obviously biased...These are interesting from the perspective that in modern Britain the interview subjects would probably all be locked up and subjected to some form of Maoist re-education.

Viewing this material gives me little hope for Western Europe in its current immigration situation. I would say that the average Englishmen of 1968 was made of stronger stuff than the brainwashed genderless masses of Germany etc. today.

A few of the places mentioned in those two newsreels were site of atrocities like the "Bradford Grooming Scandal" and the Southhall riots of the early 1980's.

Looks like Enoch was right.

Thanks. I have another link I have to send your way. Found it and lost it some good stuff....On "Negro Mountain" (though I heard it called something else as a kid...) out in Western MD. Its amazing the amount of web based screwing off I am doing right now. I've been hitting your website like a crackhead hits his pipe...In the midst of BS math shit and a two semester class called "Healthcare in a multicultural environment". The only antidote (aside from getting wasted) that works.

I read Lesser Angels last night. You keep topping yourself man. Checked on that Burroughs "trove" maybe I got a little over excited. Mostly Tarzan stuff...Tell me if you need any.

One of these days before Skynet rises we should grab a beer. Good luck with your intercostals. Not much you can do with them other than not lift anything to heavy and/or rest.

*Will do—and thanks. I'm looking for Tarzan the Terrible and Tarzan the Magnificent.*

## 'The Reeducation Camp'
## News Out of Mordor from SS Sam

© 2016 SS Sam

Hi James,

See you in the re-education camp! Should be a fun summer!

-SS Sam

http://www.washingtontimes.com/news/2016/jun/2
/bill-clinton-white-non-college-educated-americans-/

"We all need to recognize that white, non-college-educated Americans have seen great drops in their income, have seen great increases in their unemployment rate, have seen drops in their life expectancy, and they need to be brought along to the future. But they can't live under the illusion that you can reclaim a past which is just that — past. This country is always about the future,"

-Bill "El Humidor" Clinton

*SS Sam, that statement is simply chilling—and my name isn't Monica...*

**'The Angry Mob Cheered'**
**Our U.K. Correspondent on the Cops of**
**Dindustan**

© 2016 James LaFond

"You need to watch this James:

"Roughly what happened to me in that riot 25years ago. I got blind-sided while talking to a cop. Broke my nose. The cop (he had a gun) told me and my buddy to move on or get arrested."

-U.K.

Thanks U.K.

You are going to have more and more company.

I love Molyneux on violence. He ought to be caste as a survivor in a horror movie, being debriefed by the pigs just before the zeeks come back after him to finish the job.

I really liked this piece. The Best thing about the U.S. falling apart is that Libertarian twits like Stefan will gain a greater appreciation for the ever present undercurrent of aggression, that will always doom rational social schemes.

https://www.youtube.com/watch?v=_3yAulC10qI

### 'Give Me A Lever'
### Hope for Lilliputian Palefaces Overrun by Dindustani Hordes from Jeremy Bentham

© 2016 James LaFond

Gosh I feel for little Mark. As Archimedes said, "Give me a lever and I shall move the world'. Conversely if you don't have the right tools there isn't much you can do, is there?

But take heart, sometimes the short white guy wins: http://10news.dk/?p=2472

### 'In Baltimore'
### 'Where Black on White Crime is Really Nasty'

© 2016 James LaFond

This piece is an example of a report I did on a local street crime, for which the video was soon censored.

### Richard Fletcher Should Be The Most Famous Victim of Black Violence in America

By the way, the Dundalk community straddles the City-County line, with most of it in the County.

In the second news story you will see a black man in a red beret, who would like to protect these white elders from the black savages that besmirch the integrity of his race—but, The Guardian Angels are not allowed to patrol in Baltimore City and Baltimore County.

The Darwinist in me says that these whimpering whites who expect to be protected by the government should all be slaughtered by the blood mad mob of dusky fiends that hunt me and my friends constantly. Their craven pacifism endangers me—so let them fall.

https://www.youtube.com/watch?v=WTTczSGTl74

**'Micro-Businesses'**
**'The Optimistic Futurist' Francis Koster:**
**Rescuing Your Local Economy**

© 2016 James LaFond

First the concept of "micro-business" pretty much tells you that we've scaled up grotesquely.

I find most of Chris' podcasts snoozeworthy but loaded with solid information. This one fits the mold. It is odd to listen to an environmentalist talking good business sense and that is what Peak prosperity is about: addressing economics within the context of other systems, which is essentially heresy in our age. The best portion, at 22 minutes in, of this podcast , I found to be the description of what we generally think of as small business, but is in fact far below the accepted threshold in the globalist age. At 26 minutes the seafood news is horrific. This is the quite quarter od survival, and Chris' approach is probably more applicable than all of the guns, bunkers and separatism dialogue online.

Since you can't take out the globalists with a sing shot, you can at least withhold your money and effort as you drop back in to the real world out of the insanity of the global soy-brain.

https://www.youtube.com/watch?v=cHiJTQUO_sw

http://www.peakprosperity.com/podcast/98720/francis-koster-rescuing-your-local-economy?utm_campaign=weekly_newsletter_235&utm_source=newsletter_2016-06-

10&utm_medium=email_newsletter&utm_content=n
ode_title_98720

**'Dickless, Leftist Men'**
**Blonde in the Belly of the Beast: Sensitivity to**
**Women's Feelings Will be the Death of Us,**
**Orlando Reactions**

© 2016 James LaFond

"I saw this girl's video and it made me think of what
you say in this article *Hel Grins, Toothless In The
Dark*. Thought you might get a laugh out of a cute
girl going off on "women and these dickless, Leftist
men."

-Sam Finlay

Well, Sam, as an extreme rightist, who despises
emasculated conservatives, feminist fascists and
group hug types in general, I place a high value on
dickless, Leftist men, for they have thus far provided
me with considerable companionship via masculine
default. After all, the more whining sissies there are,
the more whining, unfulfilled dolls with big eyes and
fury, white 'I miss my Polar Bear Daddy' pillows might

look longingly up to their Merciless Khan for—I have to, girls, it's proper, even classical, English—succor.

The fuzzy fur pillow she is leaning up against should be replaced by a tapestry of black beards formerly attached to enemy chins.

https://www.youtube.com/watch?v=ApkyDH-d2vI

**'The One Ring to Rule Them All'**
**The Orlando Attack: The War on The West:**
**Mike Cernovich and Stefan Molyneux**

© 2016 James LaFond

This discussion on ideological globalism and the war on national identities, takes a very rational turn at 23:00 minutes when Mike takes off the gloves and breaks down the globalist food chain. At 25:00 minutes Stefan makes a nice argument for why politicians want immigrants. This is essentially a discussion on Anarcho-tyranny, which is something that I have been—at first, unwittingly—sucked into through my study of violence and aggression. 8,000 Jews have fled France in a year because of Muslim terrorism and it's not a Hollywood cause celeb? This reeks of something bad and it is not the earthly inheritance of the meek.

https://www.youtube.com/watch?v=S23A46cMlWA

## 'Hunting Dogs and Cats'
## Endtime Homework: The Fall of Venezuela & The Causes of the Great Depression

© 2016 James LaFond

### The Fall of Venezuela

700% inflation?

The Bolivar is worth less than a penny.

Fingerprinting shoppers to prevent hoarding?

Eating cats and dogs?

The nation has no toilet paper left?

What a shitty situation!

https://www.youtube.com/watch?v=nTH7-Gpr8GA

### 'The Conventional Wisdom'

What Caused The Great Depression? | Lawrence W. Reed and Stefan Molyneux

What, a British financier had a hand in the Great Depression?

At12:40 Lawrence Reed makes my favorite economic analogy—what do you do when you run over a guy with a truck. The answer is, do not back up!

At 17:00 Lawrence and Stefan discuss the actual economic policies of the Hoover administration, offering a view that is the opposite of our national myth. Red argue that the Great Depression was 16 years long.

https://www.youtube.com/watch?v=2Ce6z-u_Wko


**'Being Black is Exhausting'**
**Colin is A Great Dude, But He Just Does Not Get It!**


© 2016 James LaFond


All of Colin's posts are deleted by the pro-Dindu media. I save these listings as proof of intent on the part of the dominant forces in society pushing for anarch-tyranny.

"A female commenter in the bottom notices that they are acting like 'little girls.' Hillary and Michelle make an appearance."

-Mescaline Franklin

The little guy who yells, "I'm a right niggar!" and also complains of being tired has a point, a point that is sorely misunderstood and not apparent to Colin:

Being black is tiring, because:

Living with violent family members is tiring.

Not having the intelligence to rationally assess a situation is tiring.

Getting kicked out of your crib by you gorilla-size mamma for crying for a water bottle while she is eating skrimps with her man is tiring.

Getting kicked out of your crib by your own bitch because she wants to eat skrimps with some other nigga is tiring!

Not having a native language, but being stuck with using a language designed for other people—people who think too much and have all kind of crazy ideas about planets and atoms and other invisible bullshit—is tiring.

Spending 25% of your income and 8 hours per month trying to make your hair look like some alien fur growing out of a polar bear's ass is tiring!

Arguing with police is tiring. Those mofos don't listen worth shit!

Raping black bitches—who can fight—is tiring. You try it, cracker!

Yo, Colin, you need to wake the explainative up!

https://www.youtube.com/watch?v=o3OuEkxEI1g

### 'May the Crows Watch Your Path'
### Nero the Pict Lights the Warning Torch: Will the Dindu Hordes Muster?

© 2016 James LaFond

"I see that verdict on Goodson just got reached. May Odin grant you strength should any marauders pop up. Remember the taxi my friend. Oh and thanks for the .pdfs they were awesome. Going to buy hard copies for use in the FEMA camps."

Take Care Please,

Nero the Pict

I appreciate the warning, Oh King. I have been living the hermit life lately, finishing up these books. I am venturing forth at 3 p.m., and will be getting concussed by a black man. Oliver is picking me up and taking me to the gym. He has a fight in August and sparring partners have been slim, so will be wheeling my not very slim carcass into the ring for a shoe shine—shoes not included.

I will be extra vigilant. I have a hickory T-cane, one and a half inches thick, which I will carry for my midnight jaunt. Since school has let out, things in the County have been worse—with Parkville and Essex basically overrun with hoodrats—triple the visible foot traffic and 7 times more black on white attacks, as June of last year.

### 'When the Military Boot Crushes His Bones' The Scary Truth about Social Justice by Darwinian Thought

© 2016 James LaFond

"This interview was done in the 80s, but feels eerily prophetic. What do you think, O' Shaman of Brutality?"

"Stay frosty,"

Adam

Okay, Adam I love this guy. I hope he is still around so I can play a war game with him.

Yesterday, I was at a suburban supermarket in an upscale area and looked at the magazine rack. There was a nude spread of Kim Karjunkian, who I would be prepared to buy for about $30k, but her status as a cultural icon signals the end. In this same issue was a series of pictures of actors eating pussy, and even doing anal oral!

In a supermarket, not wrapped in plastic, not behind a locked cabinet or behind a counter?

That magazine signaled the end for me.

I think the narrator is wrong about the timeline and the Soviet goon was correct.

What do I think about this video in terms of the Cold War legacy?

Look, Adam, think of this as a knife fight. The Cold War ended with the Soviet Union disemboweled, and the U.S. emasculated. It's that simple. Such wide ranging and deeply fought conflicts result in the death of one combatant and the maiming of the other, like the Gung Fu adage about two Tigers fighting. The Cold War was like a compressed version of the Roman-Persian war which went on for at least 200 years and resulted in Islam sweeping the ruins of each nation before it. Once again, I see Islam—a medieval globalist system—benefitting from the end of the Cold War and the mutual evisceration and emasculation of the combatants.

Solutions?

I don't believe in solutions.

Time, an asteroid, a plague, things like this offer hope, which I've been bored with since I had a cop give my address to the two thugs who tried to kill me.

https://www.youtube.com/watch?v=M_v972hDynA

**From One War Zone to Another Promised Land? By John Carlisle of the Detroit Free Press**

© 2016 James LaFond

"This is akin to throwing live chickens into a pool of Alligators."

-WellRead Ed from North Dindustan

http://www.freep.com/story/news/columnists/john-carlisle/2016/06/19/detroit-refugees-sudan-michigan/85493352/

Thank you, Ed. This is a nicely written peace with little of the demonstrable toxic bias one usually sees these days. Some of these folks have been coming to Baltimore, also. Yesterday, while at the Department of Motor Vehicles in Harford County, I noticed 3 out of four of the driver's license and I.D. applicants were Middle Eastern, Latino, Pakistani, or Indian, many of them affluent, unlike those who come to the city.

The worst refugees that can be brought in are military aged males of Islamic extraction. The next worse is to bring in young boys without a father and then exasperate this by placing them in a city that has already been ripped apart by feuding between the sons of fatherless families. With this family we have both. Hopefully their patriarchal traditions and the oldest son—which the sponsors and writer do not regard openly as a man, which could be very damaging—will assert some influence over the household before the female American social workers ruin their character.

The mother seems lost and without hope.

The daughter might make something of her life.

The boys, they'll learn exactly what our masters want them to learn, for good or ill.

I see one of these boys doing very well for himself. I can well imagine that the various Islamic refugees will band together to defend themselves against American Dindus and become a local force to reckon with.

## 'THE MEDIA'S HATRED'
## THE PRIESTS OF WEAKNESS BY GREGORY HOOD, JUNE 22, 2016

© 2016 James LaFond

Gregory Hood has composed a lucid expose on what the media is and why it cannot be engaged or used as intended. As a boy, I had a visceral feeling that my parents were unwittingly propagating an evil lie upon me and that their words, which they intended to use to help me, where really chains to weight me down. My father left this life still believing in the vast Lie and looking upon me as a lost soul. But, thanks to the internet, and level-headed articles like the Priests of Weakness, by Hood, my mother—who had been charged by Society to brainwash me—is actually asking for my crackpot opinions. She has friends her age who have read pieces like the pieces that are not calling for race war and the fall of civilization, but simple rational cognition. Explaining the crux of the victimhood cult as he does, makes Hood's argument accessible to any workplace achiever in the work force, to any business operator, to the self-employed, and to athletes. I find his argument well chosen.

The Priests of Weakness—particularly the well-chosen graphic—is that type of crossover article that might open some eyes. If you know an online reader that just might have a open circuit in his panel, send them the link below.

http://www.radixjournal.com/journal/2016/6/22/the-priests-of-weakness

**Meatballs Eating Chitterlings**
**A Blacksploitation Movie Search**

© 2016 James LaFond

This could possibly be a Jim Kelly movie.

Staying up late after an out of town funeral in 2003, I stumbled across a hilarious balcksploitation movie from the 70s. A band of black heroes were combating the Italian mobsters who had their longhaired, flunky pushers on the street corners selling dope to black kids. Eventually the heroes do an amphibious landing on the Don's mansion, coming out of the water in scuba gear as the mafia guys await their spaghetti and meatball dinner, prepared by two big black mammas.

Once the evil Italians are held at gunpoint, the black heroes have a funny idea—they have the two cooks make a soul food dinner and force the suited mafia dons to eat it at gunpoint!

Please, if you know the title of this movie enlighten me—brutha!

Thanks you,

James

**Sam J.**    June 15, 2016 6:31 PM UTC

Looking around a little maybe it's one of these,

https://en.wikipedia.org/wiki/Black_Samson

http://www.rottentomatoes.com/m/hit/

https://en.wikipedia.org/wiki/Gordon's_War

https://en.wikipedia.org/wiki/Coffy

www.ingramcontent.com/pod-product-compliance
Lightning Source LLC
Chambersburg PA
CBHW070105290526
45789CB00005B/1925